I WROTE IT ANYWAY

AN ANTHOLOGY OF ESSAYS

Edited by
CAROLINE DONAHUE

Edited by
DAL KULAR

*This book is dedicated to everyone who has ever wanted to write.
We hope you read this and write it anyway.*

FOREWORD
RHIANN

Hi I'm Rhiann, I receive mentoring as part of an organization called Arts Emergency.

Arts Emergency links young people up with professionals who work in a field specified by the mentee. Over the course of a year we work together towards achieving a set of goals decided at the start of the journey. The overall aim of the experience is to gain things we can put on our personal statements and CVs in order to look more favourable to universities and future employers, to have an insight into what working in that particular field is like and also to clarify what we really want to do with our lives. The impact that Arts Emergency has had on my life is beyond words, I've always wanted to write and perform to audiences but I never thought it was a realistic career option. However, working with my mentor Dal - one of the co-creators of this anthology- has lead me to so many wonderful opportunities that I wouldn't have found otherwise and has renewed my sense of hope that there is more to life than just living for the sake of being alive.

To me, writing is an art form. Whenever you write a poem or a narrative it's like you're putting a part of yourself on the page and that part is something that comes from deep down. Despite the fact that everything is edited and corrected before print, it doesn't change the raw emotion that is being expressed. Every sentence is an indication of someone's mood, thoughts and personality at that second when they put ink to paper and, as we're always changing and a piece of writing can take months or even years to complete, when the book is finished... there's more than just a story there...There's a blueprint, a documentation of the mental and emotional journey of the author. That's why readers often feel closer to their favourite writer than people whom they've known maybe their whole lives.

I went through a phase towards the end of high school when I lost all of my creativity. Exams were exhausting, I'd taken art as a subject which lead to two years of constant criticism and pressure to produce unique pieces in a certain time under certain guidelines, over and over being told my work wasn't good enough. I need more detail here, less here, my concept was stupid, my art was confusing and I needed to start again. To this day I haven't attempted to complete a piece of art, not even a doodle because I've been so scarred and degraded by my experience. So I threw myself into my academic work at college thinking that if I avoided my trigger, I would eliminate my problem. I thought I'd never be able to produce something creative again. I couldn't express how I was feeling to my friends and family in conventional terms and so I mostly stayed quiet about my struggle, this was when I began to write again. Every time I found myself getting annoyed and fidgety just itching to hurt myself I would pick up a pen, maybe just to keep my hand occupied but sometimes I would write and keep going until I felt safe again. I've never been very reliable with diary entries and counseling appointments but taking five minutes to write a few spontaneous stanzas on a random scrap of paper allows me the instant relief I need and in the end, you can throw it away. You don't need to hold onto it, you don't need to show the world, you just need to visualise how you're feeling. Then you'll learn to see your negative emotions as nothing more than words on a page.

This anthology is so important because not only is it going to be a wonderful tool for inspiring and encouraging other writers who are experiencing a struggle in their life and helping to plant more seeds of support and guidance in the writing community, but also, the proceeds are going to organisations like Arts Emergency- which has given me the opportunity to write and therefore allowed me to have experiences that have resulted in these realisations about the art of writing and the significant effect it can have on a person's life. Without Arts Emergency I probably wouldn't have a reason to wake up in the morning. I would have settled into the mindless routine of life with no hope that there could be something more for me than what's outside my front door. Arts Emergency doesn't just take you on a practical educational journey but also a spiritually educational journey where you learn your limits, your dreams and your true capabilities. Any one who is willing to help organisations such as these to keep running and keep giving hope to people like me, has my eternal gratitude.

All of the proceeds from I Wrote it Anyway will be donated equally to two charities: Arts Emergency in the UK and 826 LA in the US, the home countries of the co-creators of this anthology. Your purchase of this book will help students like Rhiann and many more. Thank you.

INTRODUCTION

Back in January of 2018, Dal Kular and I had a Skype conversation about our goals for this year. We had been checking in every week or so about writing projects we were working on and the topic often turned to fear that comes up around writing. We each noticed fears about being seen as writers, sharing our work, and heard from others who wanted to write that these same fears had often stopped them cold on the way to dreams of writing and publishing.

Having been inspired by Kit De Waal and the attention she's brought to class issues surrounding writing and publication, we felt moved to create something that would allow others who dreamed of writing to feel supported in doing so. 'We want them to feel that it's ok to be scared, but to write anyway."

And there it was. A title. It was clear immediately that we were onto something. We sent out a call for submissions and they began to pour in.

We each work with people in hopes of encouraging

them to write. I have hosted the Secret Library Podcast for nearly three years at the time of publication and Dal has produced the She Howls poetry therapy events and open mic nights for the past year. We believe that the world can only be improved by hearing a more diverse range of stories, but the world doesn't get to benefit unless people feel permission to write and share from their perspectives.

In the wake of Brexit and the US election in 2016, the need for more stories and more voices was even more clear. We decided to produce this book not just to benefit the contributors and those who read it, but to pay it further forward to the writing community. All proceeds from this book will be split between two charities that support young people who might not otherwise have the resources available to write: 826 LA in Los Angeles offers writing workshops and courses to underserved youth and Arts Emergency in England offers creative support as well as the chance for young people to be paired with a mentor. By buying this book, you are helping the participants in these programs write anyway.

To say we were blown away by the submissions we received would be a massive understatement. There is such power in this writing, which came from published and unpublished voices alike.

In order to preserve the power of these pieces, we have edited with an extremely light touch. You'll notice regional variations in spelling + grammar, which we left as they were. We didn't want to homogenize this gorgeous chorus of voices, so these differences remain as features of the work.

We are so proud of everyone who submitted and of the project we're now presenting to you. We very much hope that reading this book will inspire you to dream big and, when it gets scary, to write it anyway.

With love,
    Caroline Donahue

1

TWENTY-FOUR YEARS LATER

CLAIRE HARNETT MANN

This morning I stood on Prestatyn beach: flat, vast and February empty. My walking boots sunk into the wet sand, cracking razor shells on the way to the waves. The sky was cerulean, the sun an amber orb. It was close to freezing. The wind whipped around my face, my hair secured by a hand-knitted hat and a scarf eight inches wide.

Tomorrow will be my forty-second birthday. This pilgrimage to the sea was part of a promise to myself.

When I was eighteen, for six weeks I lived by the ocean: Ceredigion Bay, framed by velvet green mountains and water plush with dolphins, porpoises, seals. I had left behind our terrace on a Birmingham estate plush with burnt out cars, graffiti and dog turds. There was a spark in me that had gained a place at a good selective school, but my years there had been a constant puzzle. Why didn't I want to be a doctor, a secondary school teacher, or even a journalist like the other girls? I did want to go to university though. Both my parents had left school at fifteen and for all of us university was a tantalising enigma. For them, the mystery of a university education was the gateway to a prosperous life for their daughter. As for me, I wanted to be plunged into great literature and to unlock the mystery of becoming a writer.

On my first afternoon away, I sat with a racing heart in my regulatory bare-walled room. I made my way down the corridor towards the shared kitchen. Ten steps away from the light of the kitchen's doorway I saw three figures in a closed circle, heard their laughter. They already know each other, I thought. They are second years and they won't want to talk to me. They'll snigger about me. I don't belong here. I turned back into the corridor's darkness.

Behind the locked door of my room, the small space between my bed and my desk squeezed in on me, crushing my chest and forcing out snotty sobs in gulps. I looked at my watch through bleary eyes. My parents were only an hour into their journey home. I was going to have to wait another two hours before they'd be back and I could pick up the pay phone in the corridor and call the brown push-button phone that sat on top of a pile of Yellow Pages in our Artexed hallway. I frightened my parents hard with that phone call, both with my weeping and the thought that I might so easily throw away all the dreams they had.

I did try to settle in, led on by every well-meaning piece of advice I received. It would get better. I just needed to adjust. There was a singular nightclub and a Student's Union filled with freshers drunk on a half of cider. At home I'd been drinking in dive bars and clubs since I was fifteen. I found a few more hardened city drinkers to hang with, but even they seemed so adept at the practical matters of a life at university. I shirked American history and seminars on Aeschylus. My hair was waist length and every day the wind made its nest of knots. I owned one thick woollen grey sweater and several cropped tight t-shirts. One Sunday afternoon the hunger of not eating since Friday caught up with me. In my cupboard was a tin of spaghetti and a tin of potatoes. As I poured out them out into a bowl to heat in the microwave, someone standing in the kitchen joked that it was a typical student meal. But I didn't feel typical at all.

My few close friends were deep into their new lives at other universities. My boyfriend from back home dumped me in my first week. More sobbing and panic on the public payphone. I wasn't even that into him, but I was a hundred and twenty two miles away and I hated to feel so disposable. I started to obsess over the few people who were still in Birmingham. One friend who hadn't got a place at uni that year, two others eighteen and at home with their babies, some boys I half knew that hung out in the pub where I had worked during my A levels.

Every day I wrapped myself the best I could against the fierce bite of the coastal wind but my body, my fears of not being good enough, and my utter loneliness, all of it stayed exposed. It seemed my true life was back in Birmingham, where I could cocoon myself with the nightlife, where my hair stayed smooth and my crop tops made other people gasp, not just me and my shivering belly. I had no idea where a writing life would fit into this. I listened to Smashing Pumpkins' Siamese Dream and forced my nails into my palms. Perhaps I did want more than life could grant me. Impossible dreams. Six weeks later I was living with my parents and their disappointment.

AT SUNSET I TAKE A WALK. The temperature is sub-zero now. I wrap my black wool coat tightly around me, bow my mouth into the nook of my scarf. The tide is in and I walk along the raised concrete path, sea lapping at my right, making my way towards the reddened sun.

The decision to be a writer, to spend my life deconstructing, reconstructing, understanding what has passed was made such a long time ago. It was a secret promise to myself that I have slowly shared with more and more people. Over the years I have taken baby steps. A practice of three hand-written journal pages written every morning. Home study and online courses. Blogs well-loved then abandoned. A few submissions and publications in literary journals. The first draft of two novels. Poetry collections assembled and shared with friends. A writing coaching group. This year I even started my Masters in Creative Writing. But I have never thrown myself into a life of writing in the way that I promised myself when I first left for university at eighteen. I have stayed in my home city. I have remained in retreat from that fierce bite of full exposure.

I have been married for twenty years now. Tonight we will celebrate my birthday with a restaurant meal, Cabernet Sauvignon and a hotel room of our own. My eldest son has been away at university for two years. My youngest son hopes to go away next September. Four years ago I started a teaching degree and lifted myself out of a lifetime of unfulfilling admin jobs, and now I teach English to refugees and migrants, three days a week. On the other days, I walk out into our local park and follow foxes, swans, egrets. Afterwards I write.

Tonight I travel towards the sun as it lowers itself slowly behind the distant lilac mountains. I make the decision that once the sun is completely out of sight I will turn back. I am forty-two tomorrow. If I am blessed, then today could signify the half way point of my life. There are promises I must renew.

The sun is gone now so I stop and close my eyes. I feel this moment, my life folding back on itself. The first half has been the journey out, led by the promise of this wild, immersive writing life. When I turn and open my eyes the waxing moon is on my right, the tide rushes to my left. There is no mistaking that ferocious Welsh coastal wind. It is time to journey back to that promise.

2

MY EATING DISORDER WANTS ME TO HIDE. BUT I WRITE ANYWAY

HANNAH HOWARD

My eating disorder does not want me to write. Especially not about myself. Especially not about my struggles with food. Especially not about the messy stuff.

"What kind of eating disorder did you have?" Asks a kind lady we'll call Brooke, a friend of a friend. Our mutual friend introduced us because Brooke works in the ED recovery field. She hasn't read my book yet, or else she wouldn't have to ask about the particulars of my agony. But I don't mind telling her.

We're perched on tall stools in a coffee shop on the Upper East Side. My book *Feast: True Love in and out of the Kitchen* is about many things; one of the big themes is my struggle with food and body image. Outside the window, flurries dance and people rush by, their faces lowered and tucked into fur-lined hoods and fat scarves.

"What kind didn't I have?" I've always loved food. More than loved food, needed food. It was company, consolation, and distraction. There was nothing better than visiting Mostelone Market with my mom, where Mrs.

Mostelone stretched and kneaded fresh curds into milky mozzarella, her pendulous arms swinging. If I was lucky, she'd slip me a piece of fresh, hot, weeping cheese across the counter.

Nothing better…except perhaps raiding my friends' pantries after school for boxes of sweet and salty things, gummy and crunchy things, technicolor junk food never allowed in my own childhood home. The treats were electric in my mouth. If I closed my eyes, I could feel the sugar buzz down to the tips of my toes.

When I got into the college of my dreams in New York City, there was a serious problem – I was too much, too big, too fat. And so I dieted. I dieted with all the zeal I could muster. I dieted until I fit into the slinky dresses my new classmates wore even when fall turned into winter. I dieted until I could hardly think of anything else.

My diet became an anorexia diagnosis. Anorexia! I got a job in a fancy restaurant. I learned about French cheeses and kumquats. I learned about Beaujolais Nouveau. Anorexia didn't sound right. So I binged. I ate everything in my kitchen, and then moved on to my roommates' food. Then I laced up my shoes to go to JJ's, where they served curly fries and forearm-sized chicken tenders until 4 AM. My vision was wobbly. I prayed I didn't see any of my friends under the fluorescent lights.

The next morning, I startled awake sick with grease and humiliation. I vowed to diet harder, stricter, which I'd manage for a day, a week, maybe even two. Then I'd find my stomach grumbling, my hands shaky, my fingers reaching for something definitely not on my diet, my brain buzzy with longing. Repeat. Repeat.

The woman clutched her latte and nodded. "Me too," she said. Outside, the snow began to stick to the ground. Inside me, something thawed.

When I was in the thick of my eating disorder, I had it all figured out. I would diet diet diet down to my tiniest possible size. Then, when I had achieved ultimate skinniness, I would let myself feast. After all that starving myself, I would have earned it. My lithe limbs and concave stomach would be proof of my existential worthiness.

Sometimes my fantasy was very civilized. I would nibble something I would never permit myself to eat in real life: a bowl of shoestring fries that I would dip one at a time in mayo, or a crispy chocolate chip cookie the size of my face. I would be elegantly thin in an elegant place, with tall heels and a soft leather jacket.

In other fantasies, it was all more rowdy and exuberant. A sort of low-key binge. A dinner with endless courses: cold oysters that glided down my throat, an oozing egg yolk melting atop a perfect circle of steak tartare, a lamb chop enrobed in exquisite meaty crust, champagne that sent bubbles down my spine.

When I was sufficiently skinny, when I had arrived, I would step out into the world like a debutante at her debut. Things would be glittery and glamorous. I would float atop the spell of my perfect body, my perfect life.

But my eating disorder was not just about food and my body. The unreachable fantasy stretched much farther and deeper. It was built on the premise that I needed to disappear, to hide somewhere deep, dark, and untouchable and fix myself. Only then, when I was whole and acceptable, could I emerge. Only then could I tell my story.

Feast has just come out. I wrote down my deepest,

darkest secrets and now they're out there in the universe, on a shelf somewhere, or between somebody's manicured hands. At the very moment I write this, home on my couch in pajamas in the middle of the afternoon, someone is reading about how I tried desperately, and without success, to make myself throw up. Someone is reading about how I stared myself down in the mirror, fantasizing about slicing off slivers of my thighs, my stomach, until I found myself deep in a self-loathing crying jag.

What happens to a secret when it's not a secret anymore?

It loosens its grip.

My eating disorder is cruel. One of its tricks is that it speaks to me in my own voice. It sounds very convincing. When I was in the thick of it, I believed that voice was the truth. I believed the most obsessive, small-minded, judgmental, and nasty part of myself. A big part of recovery is detangling ED Brain from Sane Brain. ED Brain is steeped in shame. It is a bully. It tells me the cruelest things about me. And even worse, it says: *Don't write. Nobody cares what you have to say. Who do you think you are?*

Sane Brain says: *Hi! I've been writing since I could hold a pen. I have a story to tell. I have a book to write.*

They argue. On good days, Sane Brain triumphs.

It's been six years, four months, and three days since my last binge. I think of ED Brain as a radio station that I have slowly, surely tuned out, with a lot of work and twelve step meetings and practice. Usually, it's just static these days. But sometimes the dial creeps back to hear what it has to say, which is never anything nice.

Writing *Feast* was hard because I had to consciously turn on the ED Brain channel. In order to write about those hard, dark, times, I had to jump right back into the middle of them. I found my heart beating fast, my palms slick with sweat, tears wetting my cheeks. I started seeing a therapist again. I took a lot of breaks. I called my sponsor twice in twenty minutes and left her back-to-back rambling voicemails. But I wrote it anyway.

I wrote *Feast* because the shame had robbed me of so many moments of joy and I didn't want it to steal away any more of my precious life. I wrote the book I needed to read when I was 18, and 22, and the book I need today.

———

Now that the book is out in the world, ED Brain wants very much to chime in. Last week, I went to my first event as an official author. I spoke on a panel about memoir. I signed my first book. I did feel a little like a debutante after all, proud and shiny.

Until I saw the pictures the next day on Twitter. ED Brain leapt into an old, familiar tirade. Why did I look like twice the size of the other people on the panel, the lovely writers lined up next to me in their trim blazers? How had I failed so thoroughly? Look at the way my thighs unfurled! Look at the way my arms squished in on themselves, as if they were growing extra arms! The horror.

ED Brain had a new line of savagery. It went like this: *Ha! You wrote a book about recovering from an eating disorder only to get fat! You pig! You monster! You fraud!*

But I tried to change the channel. I hugged my fiancé. I called my sponsor. I went out to dinner with my editor. We ate seared scallops and drank juicy Malbec. We laughed and she told me I wrote a book that had touched people.

My ED wants me to touch nobody. If I don't touch them, I can't get rejected. I can't get one star reviews on Amazon. But also, I can't be me. I can't talk on panels with my arms and all the rest of my unruly self. I can't write articles or publish a book or marry a man who loves the whole me, in my wholly imperfect body. So the kinder, healthier, wiser parts of me tell my eating disorder to please fuck off. Fuck off so we can go on writing and living. And on the good days, even though my stomach swoops out and not in, I feel like I'm flying.

3

THE AUNTIES ARE WHY I WRITE

CLEMENTINE EWOKOLO-BURNLEY

Growing up, writing seems like something people do somewhere else. We read. There are storytellers; in this country children are the business of old men and women. Everyone else is busy preaching, chasing, fighting or selling something. It Is the late 1970's. At that point I have never been alone. I am eight years old. I have heard many stories already. We don't have a television station in Cameroon until 1985 and I am to leave home shortly after the tv broadcasts start. Stories are born in the dark evenings on our verandah when thirty years after independence the dams, pumping stations, and electricity systems of West Africa begin to signal 'Repair'. The adults groan but we children find the thick nights when we crowd together, exciting. Where we live in Victoria-by-the-Atlantic the power fails regularly. At first the darkness only lasts for a few short moments. We do not bother to see if the aunties come out. The thunder of pestles continues. The women of our neighbourhood do not need electricity to pound whatever is being battered into submission in their heavy wooden mortars.

In the rainy season the wind snatches at eucalyptus and white acacia, flinging branches high into the air. Sometimes the branches land on power lines. We are glad. This sort of darkness lasts long enough for proper storytelling. After shouting out a few choice words about the Societé Nationale d'electricité, which will not send people out in bad weather to be struck by lightening, and the Minister of Mines and Power who our parents are certain owns a generator; we settle into a familiar circle with whichever of our aunties is around. I enjoy the ritual of listening to fables. I am not sure if the aunties mean to shape our behaviour with tales where beauty mutates into evil while as qualities for a wife-to-be, hard work and persistence are preferred over looks. Message received.

In the '70's I do not yet have a story of my own to tell. I am not a shy child but. Standing up to face so much attention from so many eyes causes an unwelcome fluttering in my chest. Because I leave home before becoming a public story maker, I do not connect those storytelling nights to my reading and writing until I become an African aunty myself.

There are many books at home. I start my journey from reader to writer with Enid Blyton's Famous Five, *the Beano, Dandy*, Pippi Longstocking, Huckleberry Finn, comic book characters Gaston LaGaffe, Marsupilami, Asterix, and Lucky Luke from the French and Belgian *bandes dessinneés*. There were a few steppes, some pampas and the occasional African town but looking back I think the European societies in these books were a point of reference against which I judged normal afterwards. English seems normal. The Krio we speak with such fluid ease is 'bad English', it's broken, so why would anyone want to read, much less write in it?

African books are paperback, white and orange, well

thumbed, missing pages from heavy use. The books of Heinemann's African Writers Series travel from household to household. *Petals of Blood, The Narrow Path, Jagua Nana*. There are others. Old gold inscribed or embossed creations, clothbound dusty blue and faded red, the tiny holes etched by silverfish into the pages leave me guessing at words. *Northanger Abbey, The Mill on the Floss*, bring restrictive Victorian beauty ideals into our parlour. More messages about women.

I don't know if I would have enjoyed his writing more had I had known Chinua Achebe, like Joseph Conrad, is one of the most important writers of all time. At secondary school we have Wole Soyinka's *The Swamp Dwellers,* Achebe's *Things Fall Apart*, and Ama Ata Aidoo's *The Beautyful Ones Are Not Yet Born*. The rural historical settings seem further away from my everyday than England's fields or the mountains of Middle Earth. Like my parents Achebe is mission educated. In Achebe's book *The Education of a British Protected Child,* he writes that he is brought up to read *'books English boys would have read in England."* Achebe manages to write literature in English from a very specific Igbo cultural perspective. I grew up in between cultures and read a mixture of books neither Achebe nor any English children would have. My thinking and later, writing are Krio, Sawa, Cameroon English and British.

When I move to Britain my guardian is Aunty Josephine, an avid reader, political activist, a Londoner who arrived as part of the African Windrush generation. I find this out from the funeral programme in Derby Cathedral thirty years later. Aunties do not talk about themselves very much. They do not write about themselves either. All I know at sixteen is that Aunty J always opens the front door of her two bedroom flat with a huge smile for me, on her face. *Mrs J* is the first poem I had accepted into an anthology. Aunty J. looks a little different to my Victoria aunties. She is light skinned; soft voiced. Aunty J. often has her nose in a book. She sits in a floral upholstered armchair in her small parlour. I look through the books on her windowsill, a little nervous at being up on the ninth floor of a tower block in NW6. I have grown up in a series of cement block bungalows. I remember the white metal painted single glazed window and my gaze dropping through watery light to the gray Council car park far below. Finally, I'm in England.

I learned to listen to the aunties in my childhood. There were uncles too but growing up they seemed less vivid than the aunties in their huge Holland wax head-ties and wrappers, loosely slung around their substantial waists.

Some of the aunties are related to my parents but in our little British colonial community, we are encouraged to call most adults 'aunties' and 'uncles'. English speaking Cameroonians used to be British protected persons. We live in a carefully maintained parallel world of ex-Englishness. We watch people play lawn tennis and rounders, we wear school uniforms and inherit memories of Empire Day.

The aunties generally agree on "how to succeed": a Good Education and a Good Job after that. Then, since African aunties tend to be pro-birth, a Family. We do not discuss seriously the fact that I might not want to be a parent. The aunties are hard workers, people from humble beginnings who have educated themselves. I admire them unquestioningly for a time.

If the aunties give me a map for life, magnetic North is a Good Job that pays enough to support the extended Family, a partner (husband, temporarily) and children (permanently).

My mother said about herself once, 'I should have been a writer. Then I had children.'

In my head, I heard her say to me 'If you have children you can't be a writer.'

She said, 'Whatever your job is, you're going to have to provide for a family.' That's a Black women's thing.

In adolescence I pick up on a series of unspoken messages:

'Watch out. You can't depend on anyone but yourself.'

Looking back I think some messages came from a shared place deep inside many unpublished writers.

Like this one: 'Only a Great Writer can support a family.' The flutter in my chest says 'Don't be silly, if you try that you're going to starve in a garret.' In my mind making money is an essential of being an adult, like breathing is part of living. I never actually talk about any of this with my aunties. But who talks to their aunties at sixteen? I don't ask if they have ever felt this way. I am not getting along that well with my mother. I jump at the chance to be independent, leave home.

I am a sponge soaking up all of Scotland. There is a library in my Halls of Residence. Not having a family close by I spend a lot of my evenings and weekends in there. I find *The Hobbit*, and the rest of Tolkien's Ring cycle. The stories of a hierarchical patriarchal racially separated dream world fill me up. There are no aunties in Middle Earth. At some point I will tell my own story But not yet. For the first time I face the Gaze. There are new messages.

First it's pronunciation. 'Is that an accent I hear?' I begin to think my English is unEnglish. I sort through the messages I receive; start to write them down.

'You talk a lot, don't you?' The face is unsmiling. Abashed, I put away my teeth.

She says, 'Do you have an opinion on everything?'

What I hear; 'You talk too much. Be quiet.' The flutter grows. My chest fills up with whispering twigs. I am miserable, and stubborn as hell. There is no way I am going home or admitting defeat to my mother, who begged me not to leave. She'd thought I was too young to go so far away. I dismissed her fears. I've forgotten how it was to be so confident. So self-assured it grated on the nerves. I tuck that feeling away with the too loud laugh and the too short skirts.

I recognise most of the behaviour I encounter in Britain from the English books I read in Victoria. England feels both familiar and unreal; like I've landed on the moon and found a woman on it eating green cheese. Spoken English is strangely different from the language I thought I knew already but I learn quickly.

'Is that the time?' means it's getting late; I should probably leave.

'Won't you stay for dinner ?' means, we're hungry and not sure we've enough to feed you.

'Do please stay. I insist' means 'Stay.' A year later I have made friends. When I am not missing my mother I'm happy. Still I have an internal stutter. My insecurities show up a hesitation in the smooth flow of my diction. I stop looking in mirrors.

Each year I stand in a queue outside the Aliens Registration Office for hours, waiting to have my student visa renewed. Each time I wonder what I will do if I can't show that my field of study is valuable enough to the British state that I can stay. I am not doing anything in computers or medicine. I can't imagine the woman flipping wearily through my file will see writing as a viable career for someone like me. I am having trouble with some of my lecturers. Although my vocabulary is huge, some of my constructions are eccentric. I listen harder and speak less. I am fading.

Most of West and Central Africa is in recession, after a series of deep cuts to public spending. Teachers, nurses, civil servants, street hawkers, market women, everyone is feeling the effects of salaries being slashed by up to 75 percent. Not wanting to be a burden on my family, for long periods I'm living on very little money. It's fairly grim. I'm afraid without a profession I won't be able to support myself anywhere in the world. I don't talk to anyone about this. It seems shameful. Internally I drift.

I find a job; become an accidental expatriate but don't write. It's unpaid. Then I move outside a carefully built support network and have children. Inside it's panic. Housework is the enemy and I am losing. Housework is a non-market activity. It costs me time I could use to earn merit at work. My focus on being a Hard Worker with a Good Job, a Good Mother, with a Perfect Family begins to interfere with how I feel about myself. I am not sleeping or eating well but I am managing to conceal that. It seems shameful. I have so much compared to others.

Looking back at the lost years I suspect postnatal depression. I feet hollow all the time. Everyone around me seems happy. Then one of the mums from school connects the exhaust of her car to a hosepipe and goes to sleep in the back seat. The other kids call her son "suicide boy" for years.

Over the years I had thought sporadically about Writing, usually when people said. 'You always seem to have Something to Say.' On occasion I could hear they really wanted to hear my story.

I say I am too busy to write. I have children. Keeping them content works out no easier than keeping my cool, keeping my Good Job, and developing the adult relationships I want. There never seem to be enough hours in the day. Doing something for myself seems a low priority. Two jobs and a crisis or two later, someone suggests I keep a journal. I start a meditative practice.

At this point I begin to see. I am following voices in my head. While some voices can be wise these are only afraid. It's not the aunties. It's the world speaking to a place deep within me that will always be there. When I finally begin to journal and write poetry the slam scene seems too young and masculine. I fear it's too late. I write anyway. On a visit to Victoria, I find it's been renamed Limbe after a river I used to bathe in as a child. The planners do not realise the river is a mispronunciation of Lindbergh, the German engineer who built the bridge. The map of my past is shifting. I read Ovid's Metamorphoses, one of the cloth bound books lying ignored on my mother's bookshelf. The preface says Ovid tried to burn his work when he finished it. Perhaps he heard the voices too.

Eventually through body focused meditations I begin to notice emotions and sensations in real time. A world of internal experience opens up. This is how it must feel to be an infant. When I am writing I feel calm; a settling-in sensation that anchors me to the immediate moment. My mum's voice reading to me, and my own voice as I read to daughters. The anxious messages are fading. When I write I move towards what instinctively feels right for me. No one in the books I read has the Victoria aunties. My stories connect me to other people in a community of writers; through them, to them I become one of the aunties.

On Monday and Friday, I write in a room where there is nothing to distract me. On the weekend I stay where my daughters can find me, to ask me questions about things they are thinking about like hormone free contraception, or things they have found, like confidence, friends, homework or socks. And the best thing? Housework has become my refuge from writing; writing is my refuge from housework. I'm telling stories in public and writing. I tell myself Toni Morrison started at 38. I have time.

4

OFF THE TRAIL, ON THE PAGE

MELISSA FU

When I started writing this piece, I thought I knew where I was headed. I was going to use a difficult experience as a jumping off point to get me to a place where I'd manoeuvre into a meditation on how I was able to make my way out of the land of mental despair through writing and how, by writing it anyway, I forged a path through the wilderness with a fast pen and a blank page.

The trouble was, though, the jumping off point became a deep dive. My attempt to briefly recount a personal anecdote ballooned into thousands of words about everything and nothing and still, still, I hadn't written the story of writing it anyway. That particular story will need its own telling. But for our purposes and in a nutshell: devastating disappointment piled on professional failure underscored by years of homesickness made the route to depression a short, steep slope that I slid down before I even realised the world had tilted under my feet.

There are so many roads to despair: bereavement, divorce, miscarriage, loss of a job, loss of a dream, an unutterable betrayal, a slow insistent wearing down of life's colours. Who can ever say what exact blend of happenstance and circumstance will start a personal avalanche? Whatever the paths, whatever the causes and catalysts, the destination is unmistakeable and filled with a particular kind of pain. All the postcards you send from that land cannot convey its full impact to one who has never visited, but are immediately recognised by someone who has walked those streets before. For me, it was a time where everything I thought I knew for sure became uncertain. There were days when I wanted nothing more than to disappear somewhere, anywhere, that wasn't where I was. A lot of that season is now a blur. There is much that I have forgotten.

This is what I remember: That spring, the blank page became a territory of its own. A sacred space. The wide open pages of a journal were a place to make marks, summon words, transcribe half-remembered dreams, ask and abandon meandering meaningless questions. Write a sentence over and over and over on itself until the paper gave way under ink-scored ruts. The blank book could hold it all. I didn't know or care if what I wrote was good or bad, wisdom or nonsense. None of that mattered. What mattered was that here was a place where I showed up and wrote myself towards what I desired, not towards a sense of duty, achievement or accomplishment. On the blank page, that chatter subsided. I was learning how to distinguish my signal from the noise.

During that time, I discovered that writing is a place to exist. To be. Not to explain, justify, rationalise, prepare, promote, prevent, earn, challenge, demonstrate or prove. To be.

To tell the story of writing it anyway, I decided to return to those notebooks and look at the pages of writing

I had generated in the midst of my sadness. I thought clear hindsight from the distance of a few years could show me the path where writing led through those dark woods.

What did I see when I opened those notebooks?

LISTS FROM DAYS when I was too sad to commit sentences:

thistledown, anchors, dandelion clocks, brain fog, chalk, magnets, blueberry jam, mud, mountains, pinecones, grass, dread, empty, flat, river stones

Incantations beginning with 'when' and not ending with anything at all:

When you feel broken and worried and scared
When you don't ask because you are afraid of answers
When running away only exhausts you and gets you nowhere
When guilt and grief and remorse stop you from functioning
When a black streak of anger lies between your eyes, blinding you
When sleep is only a superficial stillness over constant churning
When shame lowers your gaze so you see neither horizon nor sky
When you are so sorry, so so sorry

Mourning for a lost journal:

I lost my last journal. I've never lost a journal before, but that one is gone. I retraced my steps twice, called all the places I visited in the past week, looked under sofas and car seats. I described it in desperate detail to the barkeep at the Red Lion, to NHS receptionists, to the rental car agency customer service associate called Zack, to the guy at the till at the petrol station. No one can find it.

It was orange and had a bear on the front that said 'Be Strong'. It was filled with so much sadness. Perhaps too much. Maybe it disappeared because it was filled with words and thoughts I needed to release. It was a book where the blank page was painful, where it felt like everything I wrote down was lies and accusations and trying too hard. I don't think it had my name or any names – just a lot of sadness, a lot of struggle, a lot of trying to convince myself.

I've started another one. It has an owl on front that says 'Be Wise'. Slate blue instead of bright orange. Maybe this owl is telling me that wisdom starts with recognising how so very much is beyond our control. Maybe this is better advice. Writing is about strength, yes, but also about the willingness to enter a fog and trust that when you come out the other side, it will be with something you wouldn't have ever asked for and that now, you can't dream of not having experienced.

Longing:

I am longing for nonsense, I'm looking for connections that don't come from my head, that don't arise from putting together piece by piece the story, the narrative, the poem, the presentation. I'm wanting to be taken away by a tide of accidental language, to let words carry me somewhere, somewhere I have never gone, to bring me to a landscape that I cannot pine after, because this, this body here and heart there, this mind here and soul there, this fracture across inner and outer landscapes, this broken time travelling, this has to stop. This has to stop.

AND MORE, and more. In reading all those entries, I opened a Pandora's box and thousands of words flew out. They started swirling around my head, looping wildly, disoriented in the daylight. I looked up at this dark whirl, dreading what rains might fall, what winds gust through. I hadn't realised how closed notebooks can still contain great potency.

I wanted to write a story about failure. I thought I could slay my dragons by putting them together in the same room and fighting them all at the same time with a swift flourish of the pen. But about 7,000 words in, I realised I was mistaken. The room was flooded with heat and sorrow. With their fiery breaths, the dragons threatened to blow me into cinders.

It's important work, this writing it anyway, these ventures into the dark. But it's foolishness at best and hubris at worst to think we can waltz in and free our stories from the dragons without any risk of peril to ourselves. We must be both brave and full of care along the way. What I've started to learn as a writer is how to travel into dangerous psychic forests. That terra incognita is so very scary. I'm slowly becoming more practised in allowing my writing and myself to access those uncharted territories.

Each of those dragons guards a story that needs freeing, needs telling. I will tell those stories. But it will take some time. So I bowed deeply to those dragons, recognised their dearness and quietly closed the door. I'll be back, I promised them. Then I started this version of my essay on writing it anyway.

But here's the thing: even if you end up writing about something different from what you start off thinking you'll write, what matters most is that you wrote it anyway. Writing it anyway gives me faith that I'll write those other stories eventually. They will appear on their own time. Writing it anyway is not a race, it's not a competition. The most words don't win. Neither do the quickest or cleverest ones. When I'm uncertain, I write it anyway. When I get to the point where I realise it's not going to be a straightforward path, I write it anyway.

When the story I write differs from the one I think I'm going to write, it's a sign that I've got a live one, something twisting out from underneath my fingers, something that wants to fly. So I uncurl my grip on the reins and run along beside instead. Stories are wild animals. Why would we want to tame them? If they become too measured, too crafted, they become sterile. We end up admiring their form and structure instead of being seduced by their pulsing strength and the energy bristling underneath their words. When writing it anyway, my desire isn't to capture or control stories, but to learn how to ride them, bareback, off the trail and into the hills.

5

I WRITE THEREFORE I AM

SARAH MILLER WALTERS

I started to play with creative writing at a time when, although I didn't realise it, I had it all. After a spell down south, studying my favourite subject (history), I had returned to Sheffield and had worked in the gambling industry. I then went to work in a primary school in a deprived part of the city before moving into the charity and voluntary sector, where I would stay for good. I could now confidently say that I had seen life. I joined an amateur dramatics society to indulge my other love of drama and literature, and had praise for my acting skills. I was still young and independent. I had my own car and a mortgage for my own house in process. Twentysomethings of today will read all that with incredulous jealousy. I'm just a working class girl – daughter of a bus driver and a betting shop manager – but I had no debt from my grant-funded college years and I was never out of work; never forced onto a zero-hours contract except when it suited me as a student. What a time it was in the early 1990s.

But nobody ever sees that they have all that they'll ever need. We all think that we're missing out on something all of the time. I got to my late twenties and I was surrounded by couples. Something told me that perhaps I should couple up with someone, make life complete. I picked one from the amateur drama group. He was going through a divorce but everyone blamed her. He seemed nice. So I took up with him. And the next thing I knew I was pregnant. One life started, but as my child's life waxed, mine waned. That's where the writing stopped. The novel set in a Sheffield betting shop got put in the bottom drawer.

I was mortified by my pregnancy, but I could find no reason not to let it progress. I lived with her father and we were both in work. Grandparents offered childcare help. Everyone was excited…but I could see what was coming my way and I worried. I would have to go back to work after three months maternity leave to pay the mortgage, it was going to be hard work. But, I supposed, that was a woman's lot these days.

After my daughter was born, of course, the writing was forgotten. Even the reading stopped. I remember the sheer frustration of not being able to settle down to simply read a book. She was one year old before I got through a novel again. Life was only work, motherhood and domesticity. I did do the lion's share of the domestic tasks. Her father worked long hours in a coal mine. Physical work with unsociable hours. That, apparently, made him immune to a lot of household tasks. I had a full time job, yes, but because I could sit down to do it, then I was naturally not as tired as him (his philosophy, not mine). I did all the night feeds before dropping her at nursery at 8am and going straight to the office of the community group that employed me. You can see how all creativity was squashed into a little-used corner of my brain. Just as it started to get easier, I got pregnant again.

This is the story of all ordinary mothers of my age

group. Only the wealthy can take long maternity leaves or give up work. Only the most modern and liberal of fathers give the mothers of their children space to be themselves. I have explored my partner's attitude with friends and we have concluded that it is not entirely his fault. He grew up in a working class home where men worked and mothers stayed at home and idolised their boys. He is an only child, an only son, and his mother did everything for him. He has never learned to cook and has no intention of doing so – even though he reckons my cooking is nothing to write home about. He expects me as the woman in his life to worship him as his mother did. Because this has not happened, our relationship has deteriorated.

Because I would not worship, I started to become subject to little attempts to keep me in my place. And that did me a really big favour.

By 2008 my children were a bit easier to manage and I was getting a full night's sleep again. Unconsciously, I decided to begin to find the old me. I took a short Open University Course to get a work-related qualification. This involved an exam at the end of it and I still remember vividly the day that the post brought my results. I found I had passed and I was immensely proud of my achievement. I had worked, run the home, looked after two small children and still managed to pass an academic exam! He came home and I told him, happy and smiling. He didn't look at me. He didn't respond to me. Just gave a "so what" face and put his sandwich box on the side ready for washing. He might as well have smacked me round the face with it. I pursed my lips and carried on. If I could do that course, what else could I do next? You could pay for Open University courses with your Tesco points back then so I signed up for another. Creative Writing. I didn't tell him I was doing it. Though he probably guessed I was up to something.

"Put that pen down and pay me some attention. It's only rubbish what you're writing anyway." was something he actually said to me, once. Honestly. With that retro mind-set, he truly believes that nothing that I do or say can be as important as his words and deeds. Probably around this time I decided to put a limit on what I said to him. I had noticed that if I told him about a bad experience at work, he wouldn't respond to me directly, just counter with something worse that had happened to him. If something good happened, again – his day had been better. If something had gone wrong then it was my own fault and sympathy was out of the question. If something needed doing around the house, or the children needed taking anywhere, then it was up to me to take the time off work because he was too important to be able to take time off. To put things in context, he is now a delivery driver for an aggregates company while I work for a charity that supports people who are terminally ill. I can't really see why he thinks his work is more important than mine. He appears to be a massively insecure person and I try to be sympathetic to this…but it doesn't make it any easier to cope with. So, I have created a life that he knows nothing about, because I don't tell him anything and he never asks. I've done all sorts of things that he would disapprove of… and the best thing is I never have to tell a single lie.

I am using the present tense because I am still with him. I have decided that some kind of stable home for my children must take priority and that I will not leave until they are safely delivered into the world. Besides, I can't afford to leave him. This is where the writing comes in… and that massive favour that he has done for me. Because I won't/can't leave, I must do something to protect my own sense of mental wellbeing. He is a carbon copy of his father, and I have seen what a passive attitude to this kind of behaviour has done to his mother. She has been diagnosed with depression. She cries. She invests too much in her grandchildren to give meaning to her life. I will not let that happen to me. I carry on writing because, quite frankly, it gets on his nerves.

BACK TO THE Open University course – well, I got some kind feedback on my early attempts to begin writing again. I started posting flash fiction on a local internet forum and again, feedback was kind and supportive. I started a history-based blog – and people read it! A plan started to form. If I could only get published, I might make a bit of extra money on the side and stash it away for my escape. Just like one of the Mitford sisters, I set up a "running away account" in the Post Office. This really gave me momentum. I began to self-publish books on Amazon, hoping that either I would be spotted by an agent or sell loads of downloads and copies myself.

Of course it hasn't really worked out that way. I perhaps sell 3 or 4 books per month – just a little trickle of an income that maybe pays for my fancy notebook habit. But as time progressed, I noticed something. The act of writing itself has been my saviour. I wrote a novella where the main character's petulant husband died, giving her the freedom to be a poet and campaigner for her local community. He died of a heart attack after eating too many meat products (I am vegetarian, my partner eats whole packets of sausages in one sitting). Oh the fun I had, as the petulant one crumpled under his heart attack and the wife realised what her freedom from him meant. Being able to write things like that lowers the blood pressure. I create worlds of my own to escape to while wiping his dishes and half listening to his perpetual drone. If I feel myself becoming upset about another of his attempts to belittle or infuriate me, all I need to do is make up a new story and my anger and upset can subside. A direct response from me is what he wants…but doesn't get because I'm not really there. Writing is literally keeping me sane through this troubled period of my life. I do it because of, and in spite of, my living conditions.

When I write I am not Mum, I am not "her indoors", domestic slave or wage slave. I am Sarah.

6

IT'S ONLY WORDS

PRERNA UPPAL

I am a mass of unmet desires
Unsaid ambitions
A mask beneath a mask

A tangle of identities
Mutating, melding, coalescing
Into a mess

Every day I pick up a pen and write my laments
Every day I start afresh – different day, same story
Every day I retell the saga of mediocrity
Pining for what could-have-been

Every day I spill my ink-splattered guts
Reduced to words, my fears seem smaller,
    manageable
Buoyed by words, my hopes bob up to the surface

A mirror, and a window
Words help me make sense of two worlds

At odds with each other

I write not to please
I write unpalatable truths
I confess to sins

In words I find love
In words I find meaning
In words I find release

Whilst I write them
These words
Sustain me

This is a poem about why I write and what putting pen to paper means to me.

My inner critic has always held court in my head. Over years, his voice has been strengthened by myriad opinions of external voices, who have sometimes kindly, others not so much, told me that while I write well, I am not exceptional. Being an only child being brought up on hope for glory, not being exceptional was never an option. And so began my inner journey to deconstruct my confidence, and further withdraw inwards - my introversion was complete. Don't get me wrong, I am a very proud introvert; I just wish, I was better understood.

That's where writing helped.

I am a trained journalist, who has had her work published fairly extensively in India. But I have never been comfortable calling myself a writer, after all I have never written a book that's been published, I don't write for a living.

I am definitely not a poet, because I never learnt the form, and it was only recently that I started to read and write poetry. In a nutshell, I am convinced that I am a fraud.

However, I continue to write. I write every day. I write to understand my own self – it's therapy I administer to my self. I write to be heard, even if to my own ears. Sometimes, I write to get out of my head. Most days, pieces are extremely personal, and often raw – not for public consumption. But every now and then I create something that begs to be shown the light. This piece is one such creation.

7

THE NECK OF THE GIRAFFE

ERIN JOURDAN

You are a powder puff, a puff pastry, a pom pom, a snowball covered in coconut, you are crazy, you are half-baked, you are not complete, you are a morsel of food, an object, a thin pretty layer over a skeleton. You are wrapping paper. Your lips are a bow. You are in a box, you are half in the bag, you are not necessarily wrong but null, aging and becoming void. Half in one world and not of the other. Your answer is right but it sounds wrong. Your answer is wrong because it does not sound right.

The picture is in Kodachrome - a bright buttercream yellow of the 70s. Little flowers repeated in rows on the patterned comforter with thick manufactured lace edges. A princess four-post bed with the legs spray painted with gold. I'm sitting at a matching desk and in front of me is a typewriter. It came in its own baby blue plastic suitcase and I think it belonged to one of my great aunts – either Rosella or Bridget, who would later give me their giant clip-on rhinestone jewelry and brooches.

My father would write a sentence to start me off and then it was my turn to tell a story. I do not know how this started, because my mom was the schoolteacher and my father was not very creative. I was probably curious about everything, and the typewriter was a mysterious and powerful machine in the 1970s. This is before car phones, or VCRs. We didn't have a computer, or even a digital clock.

The typewriter was responsive to the touch and punched the paper with a smack. The crisp noise of the keys and the explosion of ink on the paper, smeared with the power of metal on wood pulp moving, the carriage advancing from right to left. My fingers would dance quickly across the keys until they twisted, and two keys would pop up at once trying to occupy the same space on the page, getting stuck. I would pull the hood off and stare into mechanical underpinnings of the typewriter's bowl of keys. They were like skeletons being asked to dance.

I wondered what words had come before from that magical space, pulled out of the shadows inside the typewriter. It was like the first time looking inside a piano, or the underside of a mattress. Seeing the bones of the machine, the parts you don't touch, the interior where the structure comes from, the keys with multiple points of punctuation. How was it decided, which letters go next to each other? Why is it not in ABC order? What is a semicolon or a slick s-like ampersand?

My father starts a story, probably about a path, or a boat or a dog. That is your world when you are young. A house or a car. A brother or a sister. A cat and a tree. There are clouds in the sky and bugs in the grass. Friends named Amy or Sam.

I've got ink on my fingers and I have to wash and scrub

to not get it on the bulbous, ivory keys. The "e" is starting to fade. Could I use it up and not have any e's left to write with?

Typing a story with my Dad is playing. Everything was play – making a cake, picking up your room, raking the lawn. Then this happened and this happened and that. Our worlds are not separated by space between words, or the right punctuation, they just flow to this and that and this and that.

I felt so proud, to sit at the desk and to be allowed to put my hands on the machine.

I knew I loved words. They made me laugh. They had little differences and characters. But I can not remember exactly when it became part of my identity. When did it bloom into a neurosis?

IN JUNIOR HIGH. Ah yes. Being teased. Feeling like an outsider. I adapted writing as a coping mechanism. I also adopted punk rock. Junior high was my entrée to the jungle after voyaging only to a local park. I'd hit the big time of teen angst and my diary became the one place that I could be free and try to trace my adolescence like an anthropologist of myself. It was a record of being part of the world - a person in my own right outside of our home. As my purview grew I had to come up with new reactions and test and hypothesize. Living outside of our house meant that I finally had my own personal drama. Places I liked to go, people I wanted to avoid, needs to be fulfilled.

There was Sid and Johnny, mohawks and Thrasher magazine. My own taste in bands and my Walkman keeping those siren songs private. I went to Japan. I had my own taste in clothes, opinions and sports.

Then writing became a way of keeping score. I wrote about the social sphere of junior high and Milwaukee's eastside punk scene. My diary was a place to write about boys and the strange incongruous policies I was learning about in church and class. I was precocious. I had a teacher ask to speak with me after class and he questioned where I had copied my poem assignment from. I started making funny limericks to make people laugh.

IN COLLEGE instead of having a diary, I graduated to a journal. I went to the University of Iowa and I had never heard of the writing program until I got there. I took some classes. Smoked pot and wrote about a girl who was hired to help an eccentric millionaire. I turned it in as a play to be read aloud. It made no sense and probably read like a psychotic break or an exotic call for help. I was reading the illuminati in the bathtub of a bat-filled flophouse and working at a grocery store as a checkout girl. Underage, I'd put a pillow under my dress and see if I could get served at the local bars. I attended the famous Vonnegut house parties on May Day with a boy dressed like Elvis.

My world was about suitcoats and plastic water guns, 25 cent draws of beer, boys who didn't notice me, going to classes that blew my mind, making snow angels on the street. At this point I was writing on a word processor, which showed 2-4 lines of text in a tiny box as you typed and you could copy your paper to a floppy and print it out at Kinkos.

GRADUATING from university I went to live at my parents' house in Long Island. In the burbs I looked for a job in the back of the New York Times. In the endless classifieds I circled things that looked interesting, completely unprepared for the work world. I had told people I was going to become…I hadn't actually thought about it. I didn't know if I was actually going to become. I was shocked as a child that people really grew taller and weren't just born their current size. I didn't get it. I was mind-bogglingly unconscious of the adult world.

I focused on the publishing industry because, well, I liked books. I got a job as an assistant to the Vice President of Marketing at Tor Books, a subsidiary of St. Martin's Press. I moved into the city and started working on the 11th floor of the Flatiron building in Manhattan making $17,500 a year and sitting outside my boss's office while she chain smoked. I made slides for presentations on an old Mac that looked like a toaster oven. I traveled to Canada and Florida. I went to the Science Fiction Writers of America Conference. I met writers and weirdos and started taking writing classes at the West Side Y.

I left and had a series of jobs from educational CD ROMS, nature videos, assisting an artist in SOHO. I worked at a literary agency in a brownstone in the 50s as a receptionist. I had never met such nasty women who seemed deeply unhappy but I understand it now as a middle-aged woman myself. Life is tough after you have been through the wringer a few times and seen the other side of the rainbow. There always seems to be another side. I sifted through endless piles of slush (which is what unsolicited manuscripts are called). I made spelling errors and I refused to clean up their basement full of reader's copies. I was fired and one of the agents called me a bitch, which I take as a compliment.

I was in a writer's group that pretty much was about eating and talking. Nice people though.

I worked at the Hearst corporation at their new internet company. I had to be introduced to the head of the division who was the ex head of the FCC. I was marched through gold and glass doors up to executive offices with wood paneling and real art on the walls. I was petrified. It was all glamorous and about sweater sets and summer homes. I was from the Midwest and had to get with the program. Later, I was recruited for twice my salary and moved to San Francisco.

I applied to graduate school and started the MA and MFA program at San Francisco State. I dissected writing, and found my riffs. I made friends and competitors, lifelong frenemies. Going to an art school meant that I was not taught how to make a living and it was considered incredibly gauche to ever discuss any sort of desire for publication or remuneration. You were doing it for the art. People got derided by teachers and left the program. A few individuals were "queeened" or "kinged" as future superstars. I met teachers with amazing powers to tap into the creative force of the world. I drank and caroused and was lonely. I wrote a series of short stories, prose poems, a book and a play. I left with my own taste.

I published as a prose poet – work one of my professors called "girlene" mostly about female desire and being a chimera. It was about blind spots and loss and female anger (which is a close neighbor of female desire). I won little prizes. I was accepted to arts residencies.

ONE OF THE strangest things happened to me a few years ago, here in Los Angeles. I had just moved here and was invited by a friend to a women's "consciousness raising" at an art gallery. I arrived late, and sat at a random table with a few people I knew tangentially. We were supposed to talk about how we felt we fit into the arts. I said I had recently moved from San Francisco and I didn't have a network of writing colleagues in Los Angeles. I didn't feel like I fit in.

A WOMAN said to me, "Erin, we know who you are. You're the girl who dated POET NOT WORTH NAMING." She said it in front of people I respected. I was wounded. How can she define me by who I dated? And here of all places? I was flummoxed, angry, and the irony has never left me. It fed one of my fears. When my muse qualities or my ability to gain attention left I would be ignored, and rendered mute and voiceless.

ALICE B. SHELDON published under the male moniker James Tiptree, Jr. In *The Double Life of Alice B. Sheldon*, author Julia Phillips reports from Sheldon's diaries, " Instead of which I was born a girl and my life has been quite different. I find myself today a young citizen with a promising future, and there the similarity ends. I have had about four different and disparate careers. I have been married twice. I have seriously upset a great many of the people who came close to me. I rejected the one child I almost had, and a subsequent illness has made it unlikely I shall ever have any. I have been called brilliant, beautiful, neurotic, suicidal, restless, amoral anarchic, dangerous, diffuse, weak, strong, perverse and just plain nuts. I have never had a "nervous breakdown" nor needed actual mental help, but I have been through significant periods of despairing confusion [...] And it is my belief that at least ninety percent of all of this has been traceable to my being of the female sex in this place and time."

Sheldon goes on to note, "I can trace out so clearly the manner in which I was derailed, time after time, from what seemed like my basic life pattern. [...] My "brilliance," my passionate intellectualism, my anarchy, are to me artificial traits, like the neck of a giraffe; I would never have normally developed them had I not had to feed on tree tops to survive."

I think most women struggle with definition. Writing and telling stories help create those outlines we can fit into. Or not. We are silenced, written out of the story, ignored and erased. When people say history is told by the victors, you know you must persist. From an email with a sonogram attached, a birth announcement, an obituary our narrative is constantly defined. I write as a way to organize my thinking, to massage my brain, to cement my ontology, to play with my interior world. I am motivated by anger for the inequality present in the world. I want to show another way to think, to live, a new line of consideration. I write to meditate, to clarify, to deduce. At this point in my life often the writing is not as interesting to me as the depth of thought behind it.

MY WRITING IS my ultimate Achilles heel, the easiest place to hit and take me down (like that spot on the dragon the fighters shoot an arrow at to defeat it). I need to take responsibility for the fact that it is me. I did this to myself.

I thought I would just get over it after a while. From writing as form of play, a form of therapy, a form of history, then as a craft of art I lost something. I have been sitting here for years with the cord unable to fully plug it back in. I let writing become terrifying.

At AWP in Los Angeles I came across an anthology I was in and I was still there. I could point to myself. That is me. I'm still here. I was not sure I still existed. And I do.

How can I evolve and adapt much like the neck of the giraffe? It is an important question to ask as I move past a year, five years, ten years of writing. A steady reminder to take sustenance from places others can't reach, and continue to stretch past what is offered. It's a call to feed on the treetops and push my creativity to survive.

8

TEACHERS AND LOVERS

CLAIRE BASARICH

Writing has always seemed like a magical activity, ever since I was young enough to appreciate books and storytelling, and all the potential they hold.

When I was little I was constantly making up scenes and adventures for my sister and me. And when my sister outgrew it, I continued with toys and friends, revelling in my imagination. I invented stories and bound the crayoned pages into little books, wrote long illustrated letters to friends during summer holidays, and made elaborate comic strips about my friends and our shenanigans.

At that point, the idea of writing as a career seemed akin to saying I want to be a wizard when I grow up. Fun to dream about, but...

Writing was never mere magic: It was concrete and real, but seemed just as out of reach.

I was lucky to grow up in a house full of books: my dad got his PhD in literature, and our den was floor-to-ceiling dusty books (primarily the 'Canon' of old white man books, to be clear). Education and reading were imprinted on me as worthwhile endeavours, but with a clear line between what was acceptable and what was not (understanding, appreciating and criticising literature vs. being a creator and writing as a fun and accessible activity).

English was my favourite subject at school, and in high school I started to become interested in experimenting with writing myself (aside from Journalling, which I had always done mainly as a vehicle of emotional venting and thinking through future goals, as I think many young women do). I started to become more confident: I had always been a writer as a child, so why not take the next step?

My young adulthood, though, was a minefield of people telling me why not.

Teachers

As a teenager, I started to take an interest in poetry, as in: I wanted to MAKE poetry.

But not the rhyming couplets kind of poetry (I'm sorry, but that's already been done: fuck couplets).

I wanted to play with words and put them together to make a kind of music, experiment with juxtaposing sounds and images that had their own strange meaning just to me; I wanted to provoke and explore feelings and ideas and stories on an abstract and visceral level. But this was the suburbs of Atlanta, Georgia, where the norm was khaki shorts, Britney Spears, Saturdays at the mall, smiling churchgoers, and barbecues on American football game days…. I was never really part of that world. I loved Tim Burton and Joni Mitchell. I had always pictured my grown-up self in a black dress and red lipstick, drinking wine and singing on the streets of Paris with like-minded weirdo artist types. I was incredibly shy about revealing this side of me, I was afraid of how raw it was, how vulnerable. I was afraid of judgment.

Then I hit a wall.

An English teacher told me one day:

"You can't write poetry until you've <u>studied all the classics</u> and understood what has come before. You <u>can't</u> just make it up as you go along. Poetry has to have a particular form and style, there are <u>rules</u>."

Cue deflating balloon noise.

FAIR ENOUGH. It IS good to read plenty of poetry to see what you like and to see what it can be. Historical influences can be part of what makes poetry interesting and what gives it weight and depth.

But the way this teacher put it, it didn't sound fun. It didn't sound liberating and exciting and full of potential, open to anyone. Poetry suddenly sounded boring, restrictive, conditional. Maybe this wasn't for me.

Later, as an undergraduate studying English Literature (though with the constant drum beat of naysayers in my head: *don't study Arts and Humanities, you'll never find a job, you'll never make money...*), I was swept away by all the possibilities in modern art, literature, and poetry. Here were groups like the Futurists, the Modernists, people interested in exploding tradition, exploding language, creating, having a ball and not giving a damn. There was even a healthy dose of wandering the streets of Paris drunk in crazy outfits.

This was a history of art and writing that I could get behind. Know the past, but don't be held back by it. The arts can speak to each other: painters inspire writers, poetry inspires music and sculpture, everyone can do anything anytime, it doesn't matter if you went to the

Sorbonne or have a PhD or have never set foot in a literature class: you just have to want it and DO IT. I loved this.

Sadly, my excitement in the creation, the art itself, did not translate to quite as much dedicated study and self-belief as a literary writer and critic: I got average to good grades, but I also spent a fair amount of time smoking, playing drunk charades, throwing house parties, dancing to vinyl records, sneaking into bars and skipping my morning classes to hang out in a basement apartment with my older, depressive boyfriend and watch arthouse films. I had started to get the lifestyle, but I was not putting in the hours. I wasn't showing up for my writing. Some may say I was making the most of Uni life, and there was no shortage of fun, but I was kind of also pissing all over the point of getting an education.

I will never forget the parting words of my amazing professor (whom I had admired so much I took all his classes regardless of what they were about):

"You are a pretty good writer, you will make a great teacher, but you JUST DON'T HAVE THAT SPARK."

Damn.

How do you recover from so much shade?

I continued writing a little bit, but privately, and I stopped thinking as much about it being a real activity that could actually go anywhere. I didn't want to continue in Academia. I was still very much embarrassed to show people what I was doing, as a writer. It felt self-indulgent and silly. I could not self-identify as a poet, definitely not.

It took some time to re-educate myself from that line of thinking.

Lovers

The best decision I ever made was leaving Atlanta at 23 to live in Europe and try to make a different kind of life for myself. 10 years later, I've never regretted the leap, and I'm eternally grateful to a family who supported my choice and all the people who helped me make it happen. As I grow older I realise what a privilege that was.

I didn't realise it at the time, but this was to be one step closer to outing myself as a writer and jumping in with arms open.

I won't lie, I was a bit of a lost young thing those first few years: starting with my first job as a pseudo *au pair* for an insane and wealthy family in Tuscany, then teaching English and living in a 7-person flat share in Barcelona. I found myself in my mid-20s scraping together a living in Spain, feeling achingly alone.

It was a ripe time for dating all the wrong men, as weird as I could find them.

One lover, we'll call him Stephen, ended up inadvertently lighting a fire under my feet in terms of coming back to writing (among other things that he was good at). We met online, and found ourselves kindred spirits as Americans in Spain looking to connect.

He helped me in several ways: first of all, I found him absolutely fascinating. He was one of the most unique and creative people I had ever met, starting as a prodigy artist and then starting his own business.

We spent many a hazy night wandering the streets of Barcelona, drinking and kissing on the beach. He radiated confidence and had built a life out of genuine passion, using his creativity in interesting ways. I wanted some of that spark. I saw what hard work combined with passion looked like.

His help came in other and surprising forms. Boosted by his attention, I shyly told him I was a writer, and one night shared with him a few of my awkward poems from high school. His response was underwhelming, at best.

"To be honest, I was expecting more from you. You are so passionate, I think you can do better than this."

At first I was furious and hurt and ashamed. How dare he judge me?! I was a kid when I wrote that. I had thought it was a pretty good start.

But he was right. I was actually ashamed because I agreed: I COULD do better. Why hadn't I? This was work I had written years ago and barely touched since. It didn't represent me anymore. I had to admit to myself that I had kind of given up: I'd stopped writing in any serious way, I wasn't editing or using my time to set up a dedicated writing routine or practice. I didn't make time for it in my life, and here I was in a city bursting with creativity, alive with music, theatre, circus and also WRITERS, and what was I doing to move forward? I partly felt so alone all that time because there had been an aching void in me for the thing I loved most: writing and creating, and a real community of writers and creators.

It felt harsh at the time, but actually his words pushed me to want to do more and do better.

I began to seek out local poetry readings, where I met an amazing group of writers, took part in my first writing workshop, and eventually began reading publicly. My confidence grew, I wrote more and I was published in local poetry journals, books and online, and eventually joined the Barcelona Poetry brothel where I got to fulfil my childhood wish of performing and sharing what I created with a group of creative and talented misfits, people with open hearts and minds.

This time in Spain led to adventures I never imagined I could be part of:

-Reading poetry on a 100-year-old Dutch sailing ship in Barcelona harbour

-Helping organise and perform at the first ever poetry brothel held in Cyprus

-Self-publishing a joint writing project with 4 other women

I had found myself suddenly brave, confident, creating, exploring. I was an adult, but I was a kid again. Fully in the moment, fully on fire.

I want to remember this period of time as I grow older and more settled, as a reminder that I do have it in me, that I can always do more. I don't have to internalise the critics and believe the limitations set by others, but I can learn from them. I can use the criticism to fuel me to work harder and keep dreaming, rather than wallowing in it and being paralysed.

Writing is part of who I am.

I am a writer.

There have definitely been times that I've felt like a failure, didn't love what I was making, compared myself to the success of others and felt I didn't measure up. It's not a perfect journey. I know that I sometimes still struggle with pain, with depression, with being too passive and not putting in the hours. I want a family but fear the loss of time, energy, identity that come with becoming a mother. This is my biggest challenge going forward.

But I won't give up. I want it to always be part of my life, in some form. Despite the critics, I wrote it anyway. I'll keep on writing.

9

A QUESTION OF TIME
FRODOT

Somewhere out there, clouds gathered. He could not see them in the dim morning light, yet he knew. Just as he could feel the wind had grown. Out there, somewhere, waves raced a gust toward the silent rocks below. There to smash, spitting salt high up the cliff. Forty feet above, he waited alone beneath the naked tree.

The tree was old. It had been there many years hanging precariously over the sea. Waiting in its own way much as he now waited for the ...

The thought escapes; I reach, but, it is gone. "Damn," I explode! Rip the sheet from the typewriter. Crush my frustration. Toss it on the pile of dead prose that surrounds the desk.

Rising, I cross to the bar and pour a stiff one. Funny, don't know whether it is scotch or rye, or for that matter care. Just something to burn the throat, to warm the body, to dim the soul. Pour another. What the hell. Who wants to work.

. . .

WHAT TIME IS IT ANYWAY? Does it matter how one moment is spent? Fleeting things, those seconds, here one moment and then gone. What would it be like to hold one, to savor its reality? That might be worthwhile. Better than plunging from one time increment to the next. Always striving, struggling. For what?

That's the real question, I think. For What. Why do I place myself on this rack of time! This expensive apartment, the sporty cars, those fancy clothes…Aren't they just things? Things no more permanent than now. Glory, perhaps? To be better known than anyone else, is that it? A year or a century from now, they'll say he was the greatest. Is that what you're after?…No. If this moment has no value, what difference is some obscure second one hundred years later. And if everyone in the world reverently whispered, "that's him", time would not change. It would still march on, inexorably plodding forward in its measured steps.

IT IS PRECISELY twenty-three steps from my desk to the over-sized couch by the fireplace in the front room. I know, I counted it carefully and even timed the walk with a stopwatch (stickler for detail). I'll bet none of the other jerks in this building know that. Having crossed to the bar, I'm four steps nearer the couch. Not one to waste steps, I pour a third and go there.

The mantle clock strikes three as I enter the room, which is brightly lit, as are the three bedrooms, the dining room, the kitchen, and even the bathrooms. I like to be up at night but am afraid and need light to keep the dreams in the shadows where they belong.

My shoeless feet sink into the soft shag and the couch yields to caress me. But I find no pleasure there, nor in the magazines strewn across the table. Dull, dumb things without ideas on their slick and colored pages. Empty-headed drivel for the masses. Empty-headed! I think, empty-headed.

She crossed from the bath in slow measured steps. Half smiling, he waited. They had dined, then danced. It was late. She came closer. He felt the urge to shout, to leap up and grab her. But still he waited. Her creamy skin shone in the dim light. Mentally, he marked the spot on her bare shoulder where he would sink his teeth. Still, he waited.

At last, she was there. Reaching out to touch, to hold, – "the thought", fleeting, quick. Too late, I snatch but miss. Once again alone in the empty room. I count the antique things that adorn my wall right and left of the fireplace, while the thousand-dollar show of understanding modern art leers at me from its nest above the clock.

I take the thirty-eight steps to refresh my drink, wondering if anything is of value. Now, I sit on the magazines, for that is what they deserve. There in the bookshelves is man's wisdom or foolishness. Whatever, it is locked in time, fixed, permanent, unchangeable. I think again of my beloved professor, a pedant of the lovable sort. Lost in his dusty tomes, sifting through a pile of dead and dying metaphors.

NOW AND AGAIN, I have this illusion. My dictionary falls from the fifth shelf and scatters its contents across the white rug. Words lie in a chaotic semicircle that seethes darkly in the center and thins at its outer rim as if the book were a picnic basket which is invaded by ants, flies, and other crawly things. Swallowing repulsion, I gather the bugs, placing each in one of twenty-six piles.

I spend hours to sort them properly; I'm careful that way. And after all, isn't there an order to things? Doesn't one day follow another? Aren't the great ideas just words in the proper arrangement? From my periodical perch before the fireplace, it all seems so clear. So logical.

Crossing to the books, my eyes savor their labels, lingering on those I've written. The seven are arranged sequentially, except for number five, of which W_ of the Times had said "somewhat obscure". That was his kindest remark! Seven also died under the lash, but five was the first victim. I select my first and excitedly reread the glowing praise.

"First book, first rate, read first!"

"... in one word, superb."

Odd, I somehow can't relate the adoration with the effort. After sweating out each line, after the labor is over, after the editor's tender loving care, its cast in type – the writer's cement. Locked in forever. As good or as bad as it will be for all time. Then it becomes a thing apart, like time. I know that I am involved but it's no longer me, no longer mine. Just a ghost of the past. Lovingly, I replace the volume and touch the second.

It was dinnertime but she had no taste for food. Why, she thought. Why? Before, they had laughed over cocktails then chatted between savory mouthfuls and later shared a comfortable quiet with their coffee. Now, she wanted to cry but had no tears. She longed for a touch, companionship, a word. Instead, the hours stretched before her like an endless empty journey.

Standing alone in the kitchen, she felt cold. As cold as he must feel lying in that grave, I think. Isn't that where it all leads? Why struggle. Why not be a happy nine-to-fiver. Of what value is this midnight vigil. When I'm dead and the maggots eat my flesh, who will remember? Who will care. And those unthinking beasts, are they so different from the lice that pick my living bones. Are they?

Time runs backward. Returning from my funeral, I wonder how I died. Was there agony. Was it quick. Does it matter. Could it have been more painful than the life that lies ahead? Dreamers say – ah, to be young. But why! Why do the old wish to be young? Don't the mountains of youth grow small. Is the wine as sweet? Memories are better left in the dark to age for, like dreams, they die in the light. What is gained by returning to some inconsequential second. A second less beautiful, less important when I am there.

I MADE a note the day Bobby Darin died. No one cared. People still went on their daily errands. Loving, laughing, cheating on another. At most, they said too bad. Ten years from now they'll say, who? I cried.

It is four-thirty as I turn from the books. I think I'll shower and watch the sun rise over the lake. I'm tired and my head hurts, a dull throbbing pain. Maybe I should get drunk instead. No, I stroll through my lighted palace grabbing a robe and start the shower.

The body relaxes, yet still I feel a tension. That unknown center is tightly knotted. The soft warm water flowing, flowing. It had been a good day. To say where it began was impossible. He tried to focus on some point in his life, some incident, some action. Nothing fit. The quandary only grew like a rotting yeast. The anger drained, poured out like sweat.

Yes, a good day. And he hoped tomorrow would bring a fresh new world for her and the kids. The rain stopped, but he saw new clouds building up over Georgian Bay. Probably rain again tonight. But it didn't matter. Nothing mattered. They were whole now, he felt it. And while he still had no idea of who he was. It seemed somehow less important. After all, she had said...

I dry myself slowly and then, robe thrown over my still damp body, I head for yet another nightcap. I'm careful not to look at the typewriter. Taking the drink along on my nightly tour of the rooms, I count the locks. One can't be too careful. I arrive on the terrace in the predawn silence. The city is still, waiting.

There is a smell of rain. It may be a good day to sleep. God knows, I need a good sleep. A dreamless sleep. Timeless. The thought can't escape. I have him! But only too sadly do I realize that I'll never catch them all. Just as certainly as one second follows another, I'll never catch them all.

THE BLACK TURNS TO GRAY. Somewhere out there, I know a new day is coming, racing to where I stand naked and alone. How long will I struggle? How much time will I have? What are those words? I ponder. Smile. As I turn off the lights I'm humming, "do un do do ... Here comes the sun."

10

RESISTANCE

ROSE KETRING

My resistance has always been about grasping. I stand grasping at every frozen thought. Anger, depression, shame fill my heart. These feelings accompany me to a type of death. There is no room for self-forgiveness.

Resistance feels like a panic attack: tight shoulders and chest. My throat closes up and it's impossible to swallow. In my mind, I feel the need to escape from what I think is dangerous. I find dark corners to hide or escape in my mind.

I was in survival mode for many years because I felt it was all out of my own control. That those people in my life were supposed to love me and keep me safe.

Resistance also feels like shame in its solid form; it lays heavy on my chest. Tears bud like flowers in a crowded room – drooping brown at the start of death.

I had married and divorced three men and didn't attend church, so I was seen as "dangerous" and mentally unstable for the children. My parents and grandparents "feared for their mortal souls." The sadness of not belonging even to a church congregation fed my isolation like a very deep hole. The label "crazy" tightly affixed to my forehead like a mantle handed down from mother to her first child.

Support

I found poetry prompts in different poetry communities as puzzles and ways to connect with other writers. For six months, responding to those prompts became part of my morning ritual before dashing off to work. Throughout the day, I checked my phone to see if comments appeared. They often did.

Many people responded to the prompts, so I visited their sites to learn how to support their work. Through supporting others work, I was also supported.

I helped create a community called the "Lone Wolf Creative Pack" on Facebook that aims to support artists by sharing their ups and downs through a weekly review based on the book, *The Artist's Way* by Julia Cameron.

Through the support of the Lone Wolf community, I set up my first newsletter in order to share and talk about the art I had created from my words. Art helped birth my words as coded messages.

It was difficult at first to write newsletters to my subscribers. I had no idea how to structure it, nor what to say. The fear of shame if I revealed something too deep about me froze my hands. Instead of writing paragraphs, I included pictures of my art. To me, displaying my art to others was safer because it was images as a form of code to my words. I opened up little by little through my paintings to my audience.

I began following other newsletters. Creators talked about change, renewal, forgiveness and compassion from other people. I began saving buckets of phrases and paragraphs that inspired me, words that could sustain when things in life seemed impossible.

Reading these collections aloud changed how I saw myself in the world. Strange at first, my tongue slowly moved around to make space for the sounds of inspiration. I discovered as an artist I am part of a larger collective, living and dead, that I can draw support and inspiration from whenever needed.

Within the books I read, I came across messages about hope, self-forgiveness and love. My own stories took over my mind for months at a time as I organized chapters and researched time periods. I even joined NaNoWriMo (National Novel Writing Month) and wrote over fifty thousand words by the end of the thirty day challenge.

Although I felt support as a member of the poetry community, I was full of anger at the memories I couldn't get rid of.

Change

My youngest sister sent me a book with meditations a couple of Christmases ago. The first time I opened it, I tried reading it from front to back but it didn't work.

I picked it up again recently with a new way to read it. I randomly choose a page and read that day's meditation. It makes me feel rebellious and able to have some control over the choice, believe it or not, instead of following by month and date. I read that passage and underline the sections that speak to me the most.

One of my favorite passages from that book is about

choosing to grasp all the painful memories from my past, or to choose Life by living for now.

"You cannot heal until you understand (and forgive) yourself."

It's been four years since I saw my daughters. I fight depression every day so that I may continue to keep my tenacious voice and heart open. Sometimes I daydream about who they will be in the future. When memories come, I honor them.

The hardest part of forgiving myself is the shame and worthlessness that come up.

In order to write and make my voice known, I have to forgive myself continuously. Forgive the shame, fear, and anger in order to open my heart. When I choose forgiveness, I accept my body the way it is and all the choices I made because those choices were the best I could do at that time. I step into my wildness and dress in Intuition and the powers of "Yes" and "No."

That's where my daily practice becomes invaluable. I know that I need to write something for at least 5 minutes a day. Even if it's just complaining or nonsense. The physical act is like a guiding light in a pitch black forest.

I've noticed that changing my attitude, how I see myself in the world, has attracted more inspiration and much less challenge. I feel more supported because I have changed how I see myself. That has given me hope and the power to keep going.

11

FOR WRITERS, TIME IS A FOUR LETTER WORD

PAULA PRIAMOS

I know a writer who is independently wealthy enough to simply leave the trappings of her life, seclude herself in a rented house someplace remote and far away, in order to come up with a first draft of each and every one of her novels. Unfortunately, my life is much more complicated than hers. I've written a memoir, a novel, and am closing in on completing a new psychological thriller, all while teaching four courses, which is considered a full load, at a local university. This means lecturing to and fielding the questions of approximately one hundred students; it means grading their assignments, too.

I've always worked full-time. Like so many other writers out there, whether they're successful or struggling to get published, there really is no other way but to keep your day job.

ERNEST HEMINGWAY once said writers must schedule a set amount of hours each day dedicated to writing, and that's a nice premise. But, in reality, he could afford to say that because in his day writers were treated like celebrities or rock stars, not to mention he sometimes lived off women of means (his second wife in particular) who allowed him the luxury of a room to himself, a desk, typewriter and a whole lot of invaluable time.

I teach creative writing at a state university and many of my students often ask me how do they *find the time* to write something worthwhile, something they'll be proud to present on the date of their workshop in my class? Like me, when I was their age, they attend school full-time and work part-time jobs just to get by.

"Please stop your whining," I'll joke with them, "because you're now *wasting my precious time*."

I'm a little tough on them because writers must have ironclad backbones. We must withstand constructive criticism, rejection or worse - flat out being ignored. If lucky enough, we see our work published whereby there are book readings and other literary accolades. But there are some reviewers, the negative ones we obsess over, who might offhandedly criticize all of our hard work for kicks, not taking the time to comprehend the intricacies of plot, character and language that we, as writers, belabored over and over again when crafting our stories. We must brace ourselves for them, too.

As for where and how to find that elusive time, I tell my students, "You just do. Ruin your social life. Forget going to that party on Saturday night. But don't stay home and make the mistake of turning on the TV for background noise while you write. And, for the love of God, stay off the Internet. In fact, hide your phone in another room."

Once they've created that special time in which to write, now do something about it. Put something down on paper or input words to fill that blank screen. Just hurry up and fail. If you don't have any words down on the page, you have nothing to work with. Writers block is for the weak.

FOR ME, once I'm in the throes of creating a new book, a haunting takes place in my head. The characters I came up with won't leave me alone. I see their stories play out over and over when I'm in the middle of teaching, cooking dinner or during a movie with a friend. The only way to make the haunting stop is to sit down and give them what they want - I finish telling their stories.

I wrote my first book, a memoir, in about ten months, my first novel that came out last year I completed in around the same amount of time too. The hours I worked on them weren't rigid. They were absolutely irrational. I remember writing two chapters of my memoir during one entire Saturday I had free. The ending to my novel I came up with at four in the morning on a weeknight when I had to teach a mere few hours later that day.

AS FOR THIS new book I'm working on, I'm not counting how long it's taking me to write it because it's not about a timetable. Nor is it about a stringent schedule that, given the demands of my daily life, proves implausible to keep up. It's about writing any chance I can. It's about reminding myself that the process of writing makes me feel like I'm doing what I'm supposed to be doing with my life. In the end, for the writer, it's one of the best ways to spend that sacred four letter word we call *time*.

12

A WRITER'S TALE
GRACE WARD

Back in 1965, when I was not quite eleven years old, I sat the Eleven-plus examination all by myself in the school hall. Worse things have happened, you're probably thinking, but for a ten-year-old recovering from the 'chicken pox,' this was akin to sitting in the dentist's chair waiting for the drill. Nervously, I began the paper by picking out the easier questions, now and then chewing the end of my pencil while glancing up at the school clock. When the allotted time was up, the headmaster came in, silently collected my paper and sent me out to my mother, who was waiting outside in the corridor.

As we walked home, Mom kept asking me how well I thought I'd done, but I kept quiet. I knew that I hadn't finished the paper because I'd become stuck on one question and run out of time. This played upon my mind, so by the time my results letter dropped through our letterbox, I was full of angst. My dad, serious as a vicar at the graveside, opened the envelope.

"You've failed," he said. His tone was flat. I sensed his disappointment, for I'd joined the thousands of others branded as academically inferior. "Obviously," he said wryly, "you don't take after me on the brains front!"

ALL TOO SOON, I was segregated from the 'bright' kids, the crème de la crème, who were being handpicked for grammar school. For me and the rest of the 98% of kids in my year who failed the examination, the future seemed bleak. We were sent to the local comprehensive, where we were put into classes where pupils weren't allowed to sit any GCEs (forerunners to GCSEs). The Eleven-plus had marked us out as middling to low-achievers, so further exams were probably considered pointless, both for us and for the school. We'd had our chance at glory and we'd flunked it. Interestingly, the percentage pass rate in other local schools, particularly those in the more affluent areas, was far higher – nearing 100% in some cases.

Had I known about the discrepancy between school results, I might have felt better about myself. If some schools could achieve such good results, why had ours performed so badly? I knew of only one boy in my junior school who'd successfully passed the examination, so that speaks for itself. It couldn't have been because every single child (bar one) was of lower ability than those in other schools. No – it pointed to the fact that these were better schools – better at exam preparation, or simply better at teaching!

Meanwhile, my confidence had plummeted, along with that of many of my classmates. Yet we hadn't expected to pass, if I'm honest. Most of our parents hadn't had the benefit of a decent education. They'd been brought up in wartime, when things were disrupted by conflict and working-class people still 'knew their place,' which, in most cases, was on the factory floor or serving behind a counter.

Now, it seemed that a new generation, made up of their sons and daughters, was also about to be written off. My fellow classmates and I had been officially informed that we were all losers, academically-speaking. Yet, I was luckier than some, for when I was thirteen I passed the entrance exam to a technical college. So, all isn't lost, I thought. Perhaps the educational establishment was correct in assuming that girls like me were more suited to secretarial or nursing careers that were relatively low-paid but thought necessary to keep the NHS and businesses running smoothly.

LEARNING how to write Pitman's shorthand and to type at speed had never been a dream of mine, but at least these skills were transferable. If one organization didn't suit me, I could utilize the same skills in another. Moreover, for a northern working-class girl, working in an office seemed a step up from shop or factory work. However, office work proved quite repetitive and boring, and it wasn't until I began working at the local university that I began to realize how limited my prospects were. By this time, I was eighteen (the same age as first-year students) and of them, I was envious. They seemed to have such a wider range of opportunities than I'd had; some lucky students had even taken a gap year to explore the world. Compared to theirs, my own confidence was at a low ebb. They were, I believed, much brighter than I was. That old chip on my shoulder had wobbled a little but stayed firm.

WHAT HAPPENED NEXT? Well, married life got in the way of my ambitions as I fell in love with one of the students and we married as soon as he graduated. We had two children, and for a few years we lived in Africa, where I found a job as a kindergarten teacher at an international school. To apply for this position, I was told to write an essay on the best ways to educate young children. This meant visiting libraries to study books and articles about child development, which I found fascinating. Eventually, I came up with a scheme of work based upon play and exploration, with examples of activities to suit different abilities. This included monitoring pupils and recording information to enable me to report back to parents. How lucky was I that the school accepted me upon this basis, despite my lack of formal teaching qualifications! The headmistress was prepared to take me on solely because of my enthusiasm, drive and initiative. I was determined not to let her down.

The school had a wonderful atmosphere and catered for children of different nationalities and varying levels of ability, including children with learning disabilities. The level of satisfaction I received from watching Chiru, an autistic girl, blossom into a happy child was incomparable. She'd arrived from a mental institution and would repeatedly bang her head against the wall in between walking backwards and forwards in an agitated state. Now, she was calm and would often echo my speech, including my Yorkshire accent, which some people found hilarious! At last I'd found work that was truly fulfilling. One day, I thought to myself, I'll return to the UK to train properly, as a teacher.

AFTER A COUPLE OF CONTRACTS ABROAD, we came back to live permanently in the UK and I worked part-time as a secretary, taking GCSEs in my spare time. When I'd acquired five, including English and Mathematics, I applied to join a further education programme, so that I could apply for a degree course in education. At first, the university turned me down as they said that I may not have 'the capacity for study at a higher level.' I remember cringing with embarrassment as I left the interview room. Still, I'd no intention of giving up – not after all my efforts! Luckily, because of my job at a local council, I was able to sit for the Higher National Certificate in Public Administration. Once I'd acquired this, I reapplied to the university. This time I was successful.

It was a momentous occasion for me when I was finally awarded a 2.1 (Hons) degree in English Studies followed by a PGCE, but my husband didn't attend either ceremony. He was resentful because I'd had to give up my job to take up full-time study, although in those days, students received a maintenance grant that amounted to almost as much as I'd earned previously. I now believe that because I went to university, the balance of my marital relationship altered. I was becoming more independent and outward-looking, rather than focusing upon the family. The situation culminated in a divorce just a year after I graduated. So, it was with a heavy heart that I undertook my first teaching job at a secondary school in the Derbyshire Dales. I taught there for four years before converting to primary teaching which I enjoyed more, because it meant teaching a whole range of subjects, rather than just English Language and Literature.

Realizing my true academic potential has been tough and not without emotional and financial cost, but the lack of support and resentment from my husband shone a light on the inequality within our relationship. Now I had to learn to fend for myself. Yet, along with the sadness of marital breakdown, came new beginnings. I was at last acquiring more confidence and mixing with people who saw me as something other than a wife and mother. Added to this, my teaching career proved far more interesting and challenging than any of my previous jobs and brought me into contact with people with similar interests.

In 2012, I returned to university to study for my Masters' in Creative Writing and I've been writing ever since. I still enjoy attending courses and run a writers' group in my local area. At present I have three novels in the pipeline – one aimed at children and another two for adults. It's been a bumpy ride and there were always going to be bruises along the way, but I'm thankful to have the freedom to make my own choices, rather than having them made for me. I don't regret the path I've chosen one bit. I only wish I'd been able to choose it earlier in my life.

So, my message is – anyone can realize their dreams and ambitions. If you're determined enough they can be fulfilled, despite the obstacles and pitfalls that may occur along the way. When I first started university and my confidence was very low, my tutor's advice was simple: 'Just keep turning up and you'll be okay,' he said. Well, I've remembered those words ever since. Whether it's the unfairness of the system, or whether it's other people who make you doubt yourself, remember to ignore that nagging voice inside your head that says you can't do something, and just go for it!

13

YOU ARE MY EDITOR

TANYA LEVY

Writing through My Rejection

I sat in the coffee shop with my friend chatting and catching up. She said to me, "I am working on a goal-setting workshop and when I am finished I will send it to you because you are my editor". I told her, "No problem," and smiled. I liked to know she saw me as "her editor." I leaned into this new story, that I was a good enough writer to be a good enough editor. It had not always been that way. As you would expect, the journey to be a good enough writer is not a straight line.

On the way home, I started thinking about my early educational career when I started in Public Relations. At the end of second semester my teacher said to me, "you can't write and if you don't do something about it, you are going to fail university. You should write and read as much as you can". I was shocked. I thought I was a good writer. I had always received positive responses on my written work in high school and people had loved my poetry. I did end up leaving the Public Relations program to pursue a career in Social Work. However, my identity as a writer was shattered. I was only eighteen when I received that feedback, but it stayed with me for years. Even now I feel blocks come up as I write.

BLOCKS for me show up as my inner critic. I can hear myself saying inside my head, "Who am I to write this book? Who will even read it? Do my words matter?" I have found the most effective antidote for writing blocks is showing up at the blank page or computer screen. Each time I show up, I need to keep writing. I have found morning pages, or in my case it is usually evening pages, helpful. This is a free writing practice that Julia Cameron introduced in "The Artist's Way". I write about it all. I write on the topic I am writing. I write about the resistance. I write my feelings. I write to my inner critic. I write against my inner critic. I write and write and write.

If I can't show up and write, because sometimes it is too hard, or it hurts too much then I move. I clean my floors with the intention of expressing my feelings. I sort my feelings out with a walk. I have coffee with a friend or talk to my husband. Eventually it gets a little easier, hurts a little less and I find my way back to the page, back to myself. Sometimes I ask myself, what story is standing between me and my writing? Is it the story the teacher handed me many years ago that I can't write? Is it a story that my voice doesn't matter? Is it the story that writers don't make money, so I should do a "real" job instead? These stories can eek into our consciousness, become stuck in our tissues and start to become beliefs that become actions and suddenly I realize I haven't written anything for a month.

. . .

Here is an excerpt from my journal I wrote in January 2018:

> *"Please forgive me for falling short, for not being, doing or having enough, especially not doing enough. Please forgive me for poor choices and unkept promises. Please forgive me for self-judgement and shame. Please forgive me for comparisons. Today I honour you with self-love, self-compassion, self-acceptance and letting go of all that no longer serves me. I focus on today."*

Do not misunderstand me. I thank the teacher now for her honesty. At the time, I remember feeling confused and lost. I think this is where my belief of not being good enough began. I did read a lot and write a lot. I learned that what she meant was that I was unfocused in my writing. Self-doubt still crept in. Remembering how impacted I was by the teacher's remarks now is a reminder. A reminder to take feedback if it is helpful and to leave it if it is not. Her feedback helped me be a more attentive reader and I noticed whose writing I liked and appreciated and whose writing was unfocused and not very good.

I also learned that having another define me as a writer wasn't helpful. When it comes to education, our teachers evaluate us, so it is hard to get away from feedback. Yet feedback still need not define us. My identity as a writer is sacred and belongs to me. It is my place to find my specific way of communicating as a writer, and my one true voice. In the same way that others do not define us it is important not to compare ourselves either. My lifelong love-hate relationship with self-doubt means that my tendency to compare myself to others can show up way too often.

I learned that my life echoes my writing and my writing echoes my life. If I am unfocused and distracted in life it will show up in my writing. Writing takes a lot of trust. Trust that when I show up at the blank page I will have something to say. It doesn't matter if what I have to say is profound or even helpful or interesting. What matters for me is the visceral process of writing, placing thoughts, feelings and words to paper. Sometimes one word spills out and waits expectantly. Other times it is a torrent that flows and flows. The act of expressing self, myself, of finding a way through the feelings and thoughts that build up within.

Writing through My Grief

Writing my feelings was never so necessary as when I lost my Mom in 2015. I had to find a way back from the dark and painful grief I was feeling. When she died, I went through a very difficult time emotionally. I wrote a poem to get my feelings out called "Sometimes."

Sometimes

> *Sometimes the heart*
> *cries and cries and cries*
>
> *Lost within the labyrinth*
> *of daily obligations and deals*
> *Doing what needs to be done*
> *Tears washing away any*
> *ghost of a smile*

*sometimes the heart
believes and believes and believes*

*in miracles of grace, hope and ease
in a new day dawning in life
and then when all is lost
counting the cost of each new day
with weary hands and eyes*

*sometimes the heart
shouts and shouts and shouts*

*ghosts of the past
removing all hope
tired from the toiling
dry to the bones
seeking a moment of silence*

exiled, drained yet never alone

*sometimes the heart
aches and aches and aches*

*burying its dull rhythm
against the staccato of wild's
relentless torment
longing for an acre of space
and a moment of grace*

*sometimes the heart
bleeds and bleeds and bleeds*

*seeking just to know
its needs*

and the subtle sadness of
a lonely boundary
each time a stronger stand

sometimes the heart
stretches and stretches and stretches

knowing it will never be enough
even when there is no other way
finding the love for one more day
when the journey seems long
and the love already lost

sometimes the heart
rests and rests and rests

holding onto a tiny seed
plunked in heartbreak's soil
Tended by unexpected miracles
and the gift of each moment
Surprised by another's kindness

sometimes the heart
knows and knows and knows

what is true
what intuition speaks
and bides its time
the harvest to reap
love need not weep
from its burden deep

I was stuck in my own loss and writing was a way through the shadow, the darkness, the abyss. It is also a way through the joy, happiness, and celebration. My mother came to me in the shape of a cloud soon after I wrote this poem, which led me to write another, more hope-filled poem.

She is all that and more

> *Struggling with my need for rest*
> *as others yell loudly for my help*
> *she comes to me*
> *I have you, she says*
> *you are all that and more, she says*
> *There is a healing going to happen, she says*
> *Trust the mystery all around you*
> *Did not I come to you on the clouds*
> *to remind you*

There was no one moment when the grief got easier. It was many moments, stuck together. Some were happy, some were sad, some were lost and numb. As a writer, my way to cope with grief or any emotion, is to keep showing up at the page and writing what I am feeling. It is all about the allowing. Allowing all of it.

Allowing was never so hard as a year ago as I stood by my father's hospital bed knowing he was moments from taking his last breath. He was my rock, my strength and my best friend. He had the biggest heart and I loved him so. Here is a poem I wrote about that great loss:

The Best of You is Right In Front of Me

*I stood in the kitchen with tears streaming down
   my face
I said to him, "it isn't fair, when I return from visits
   home
I am exhausted and you always get the worst of me,
   I am sorry"
He looked at me and said, "The best of you is right
   in front of me"*

*When students show up at my door, they tend to
   start with apologies
"I am sorry I am…anxious, sad, behind, missing
   time…"
I tell them, in different words, the best of you is
   right in front of me
For noticing where we are is the place to begin*

*How many times have I told a student
It is okay to cry, crying is a release
All feelings are okay, no apologies necessary
This is a safe place to learn and to be*

*Grief is a great teacher and I am a humble student
It taught me that one line on a Facebook post
Can heal a great aching loss
The line was, "there is no pain in heaven"*

*My father was so beautiful on the day he died
Wordlessly he slipped away surrounded by family
He was a radiant sunrise in my life
And he passed to a sky filled with a golden sunset*

It is true that we are in the business of learning and
We focus on the learning in the classroom
As we should and yet
My biggest learning this year has happened outside the classroom

I learned that when the depressed face of grief showed up
And I struggled to put on my socks
I could still get up and put one foot in front of the other
Because people were watching me and counting on me

I learned that when the anxious face of grief showed up
And I wanted to cocoon myself in my house with ice cream,
If I could even eat; phone calls,
lilacs and honeysuckle bushes sustained me

I learned that when the silent face of grief showed up
And there were chasms of pain to cross
Tomato plants, acorn squash and recipes spoke for gardening is a universal love language

I learned that when the memories showed up
And holidays approached, any special day
It helped when someone who loved me told me
"you are perfect just the way you are"

Quite honestly, I am not interested in a world
Of perfect people who always have it together

I like the messy middle, the grey, the dusk
I have lived long enough to know

When the sky is darkest, the clouds will move for the sun is never broken
The moon will wax and wane over any heart ache
There is no light without shadow
No victory without cost

I have learned to pass on the legacy not the pain
To bear witness, to be a presence
I don't remember what was said to me when my Dad died
I do remember who called me, who listened, who "saw" me

To be a healer is to see and be seen
To be a teacher is to listen and be heard
To be a lightworker is to know and to be known

Even on the grumpy days
Especially on the grumpy days
Even on the messy days
Especially on the messy days
Even on the dark days
Especially on the dark days

For I have learned that
If I give voice to my grief,
My pain, my hurt, my anger,
My sorrow, my story, my journey
Then I free the space for you
To give voice to yours

As the grief lifts, when the moments of light appear
And I feel safe to share my joys & triumphs
Please join me and celebrate yours as well
For we are all on this journey together

Healer please heal us every day
Teacher please teach us every day
Light please find us every day

For the best of us
Is right in front of us

———

WORDS HEAL US. Keep writing. The world needs your voice, your wisdom, your words. Make space and time to write. Create your identity as a writer. Find your one true voice as it ebbs and flows with the happenings of life. The world needs you. I need you. And writers, we need each other.

14

WRITING (AND DANCING) AS A RESPONSE TO DIAGNOSIS: FIGHT OR FLIGHT?

KATE SWINDLEHURST

I was diagnosed with Parkinson's in 2004. After the initial shock my response was to fight it – I wasn't going to let a disease get the better of me. What that meant in practice was keeping it under wraps and carrying on as normal. I ran myself ragged until I was exhausted, making sure I hid the condition from view, desperate to prove that I was coping, that I was as good as I used to be. When that was no longer sustainable, it was a time for giving up – running, teaching, even dancing.

WHAT HAPPENED TO CHANGE THINGS? In a way I took flight, from rural Cumbria to central Cambridge, from the public face of teaching to the private world of the writer, where I discovered a different way to respond to the condition which had altered my life so radically. Rather than denial, I would try exploring and embracing: I would take refuge in what had been a lifelong habit of reflection and invention, translating my own thoughts and experiences into stuff that others might, just might, want to read.

Except the writing life is anything but private, of course. I still remember the terrors when a piece I'd written was first subjected to the combined examination of a group workshop, the delight when I had a story published for the first time. Anyway, a year camping out on my brother's couch helped me complete a creative writing MA and win an Arts Council Escalator Award for emerging writers. And I emerged! A research trip to Argentina, a first draft of a novel dealing with the disappeared, and interest from agents and publishers at the Escalator Showcase were the evidence: this was it. I was a writer. I had arrived.

THE NEXT EIGHT or nine years followed a path familiar to many: a laborious rewrite of the novel, a "nearly but not quite" response from publishers and the advice to "put it in a drawer and get on with the next". The next was a new departure, following my interest in the natural world and its importance for a healthy life: a residency at the Botanic Garden in Cambridge, also supported by Arts Council England, and a short story collection inspired by the garden. I had some luck with individual stories but no success placing the collection.

2015: Suddenly it seemed as if half the world was on the move. Horror and disbelief combined with visits to the Calais camp with local volunteers to prompt a return to the political and the seeds of a new novel, set in Bulgaria, based on our responses to the refugee crisis. *The Station Master* won a full manuscript appraisal in a competition for new writers with the sobering result: more rewriting!

Meanwhile, I still had Parkinson's, of course. In

Cambridge, though, I'd rediscovered my passion for Argentine tango and found others keen to explore how a dancer with the condition could be helped to dance well. This was the start of a seven-year odyssey in the company of two tango teachers who eventually became close friends. I'm not sure at what point this became an exploration of the therapeutic potential of the dance or quite when our early interest in the research became an article and then a book. Through these fellow travellers I learnt that, as in writing, in Argentine tango there is nowhere to hide. If you try and dance with some part of you kept in reserve, you are wasting your time. What begins as a private passion exposes you. The cracks in your armour spread until you are all soft underbelly, vulnerable to any sword. Somehow I knew intuitively, that it was where I was weakest that I might find strength.

I make it sound easy. It isn't! Argentine tango is the hardest dance in the world and a harsh mistress (not unlike Calliope, chief muse and traditionally a writer's inspiration). But the more I danced, the more I benefitted from the tango 'treatment', the more I wanted to share the incredible news: that tango can impact hugely, not just on the physical symptoms of Parkinson's, but on the emotional and social aspects, on mood and outlook and quality of life. It transforms the dancer, from the infelicities of the condition into something approaching grace; as if my clumsy feet have learned to take flight.

A WRITER? people say. How lovely! So where can I buy your books? I watch their eyes glaze over when I reply and wonder if I'm any further forward. How will I ever emerge fully? Most days I answer my own question: just like walking, one word then another. I'm heartened by the words of a favourite author, Jonathan Taylor: "Never liked the term 'Masterclass'. There's no such thing as a 'Master' of writing. We're all beginners always." As in tango…

15

DO I EVEN LIKE TO WRITE?

SARAH SKOTVOLD

Writing is weird. I think about writing every day. Mostly in that I'm telling myself that I should be writing. But I'm not.

Instead I am organizing, clutter clearing, looking up recipes, coming up with endless lists of creative ideas for work and my personal life. Basically, I'm doing anything other than writing. But you know what I'm doing while I'm doing each of these activities: thinking about writing. It's pretty mentally exhausting.

After spinning in mental circles day after day, I have to ask myself honestly, do I even like to write? I think I do. I would love to have more confidence when I say that. Let me clarify.

I know I like to tell stories. That is my talent. Whether through talking, acting, writing, video, photos, I know I can communicate a story. I like to make people laugh. And I like to share ideas to help people improve their lives.

THE THING about writing (or acting, or photography, etc.)

that is so challenging, is there is always more you can do, your creation can always be better. Always. This gets me stuck. "I can't do this or that until I know or have this or that...." There is a constant road block, every day. There is always something else I think I need to really understand, or have completed, or have together before I start to write something. The thing is, if I wait to communicate until I have it all together, it will never happen.

So how can I ever finalize anything? I can't speak for others but I personally need to look at everything I create as a work in progress. Even if it's not perfect, I need to start to share it, so I can make the next piece better. I also need to remind myself that what I am creating is not for everyone and that does not matter. If there is one person who finds it helpful, useful, or interesting, then I have done what I need to do. I am not communicating with everyone. I'm communicating with someone. That perfect someone who will receive the information I created, just at the perfect time when they need it.

THAT'S REALLY what it is about. Being authentic, sharing my creativity, no matter what, no matter where I am, so the message can be heard by whoever needs it at that moment. Even though I know this, doing what I love and doing what I want to do is often painful because I would truly rather be doing anything else at the moment. It's the reward, the feeling after I've followed through and completed a piece of writing or any other creative project that makes me feel good and accomplished (if only for a minute or two).

I am not a great writer, but I am a story teller. I will continue to tell my stories in any way I can because that is what I do. That is all that I can do. If you can relate to what I'm saying then I have a recommendation for you, a must-read if you haven't already read it: *The War of Art* by Steven Pressfield. The book is a collection of reminders that doing what you love isn't always easy. In fact, sometimes it's extremely challenging because you can be met with so much resistance. The thing is, this resistance is often self-created and can stem from deep rooted fears and perfectionism.

I like the book because I enjoy hearing about this great resistance from someone else. For me it's a reminder that resistance is in each of us and I am not alone. It helps me to focus, get back on track and remember that I have a duty, not only to myself but to the world, to live my truth and be as authentic as possible. A calling to face my fears and push through even when I tell myself I can't, because I know my purpose is to share my unique gifts and talents, whatever they may be. I hope you know that's your purpose, too.

16

WRITING IS A LONELY OCCUPATION

DAVID ROCKLIN

Writing is lonely because we need it to be, to get to the places where the stories live.

Yet even as we isolate ourselves, we want others around us. Readers and audiences, clearly, and fellow writers to commiserate with until it's time to go away again. We're constantly living somewhere on this strange continuum, pushing the world away in order to create something good, then grabbing for the world again, trying to make it come back to us.

Maybe the wisdom about writing being a lonely occupation is incomplete. Maybe, writing is a lonely occupation because we make it that way, until we need to unmake it.

I'VE ALWAYS CONSIDERED myself an outsider. I never fit anywhere that I could easily see growing up. It was why I ended my days writing in my journal. I didn't know how to make sense of the world, let alone find place in it, without following words. If not to the end of my solitude, then at least to the saying of it – I'm alone. Writing out some version of those words allowed them to live, and the fact that they lived meant they weren't forever and could one day die. I had no idea how, and never suspected that the writing I used to understand how I felt would be the instrument of changing how I felt.

I wrote my way into adulthood. I moved from the city I grew up in because it didn't seem possible to write anything but "me" while still living in the place that shaped me. I didn't know what sort of writer I wanted to be, only that I didn't want to be the kind that only wrote and rewrote versions of my own story.

I TRIED and failed over and over. My first attempts at writing were mannerisms of other writers, not my own sensibilities. The first novel I completed was a 1,000-plus page horror opus with the Passover story as its jumping off point. (I wish I was kidding.) Stunningly, no agent reached out to deliver literary stardom. I know, right? Philistines.

No one likes rejection, but what I lacked in confidence, I made up for in relentlessness. Even poor efforts held palpable hope of getting better. The next novel was a thinly veiled account of me, written as much to get it out of my system as to get published. But it also marked an important first step: I took it to an advanced writing workshop, my first time among other writers.

I don't have an MFA and I wasn't part of any literary community. I didn't know any other writers at all. Now I was in a room full of them, talking about our work, sharing excerpts and giving each other constructive criticism. Well, mostly; some of the writers seemed to relish taking others apart for everything from syntax to substance, while other writers seemed helpless to separate their self-worth from their sentences. There were tears, fights, a departure or two.

I loved it.

———

Sure, hearing critiques of my words challenged me, but I felt close to those people because they were trying to do what I was trying to do. Taking moments – mostly from their own lives, as was I at that time – and writing to make sense of them. No, more than that. Writing to relight those moments, so they'd illuminate the moment they were in now. We had something so elemental and hard and important in common. It took me a while to find my voice in there, but the notion that I might be a writer worth reading seemed less improbable.

While I didn't find a long-lasting community of writers from that group, I did get a mentor, lifetime friend, and my first true connection to the notion of a lit family. She led the workshop, gave me honest and encouraging notes on my novel, and remains in touch with me to this day, cheering me on book by book even as I cheer her on. We're peers now, and through her, I came to my agent, and to publication. Seven years intervened, though, between the workshop and the moment my work found a home. During that time I wrote alone, still. I wasn't a published author. I felt I had no business seeking a community I didn't possess the bona fides to join. I didn't belong.

Then came my first novel, *The Luminist*.

THE WOMAN who formed the factual basis for the central character was an outsider to both her native British and adoptive Ceylonese cultures. She found, in the early age of photography, a vehicle for the transgressive need to hold a moment still and keep it eternal. She also fought for place among the completely male-dominated circles of art and science. Of course, I had to write about her when I came upon her work at the Getty in L.A. She reminded me of me.

THE LUMINIST GOT me an agent and was sold for publication. The dream, happening. The subsequent book tour put me back in the company of writers for the first time since the workshop seven years before. Spending time at readings and events with writers gave me that sense of belonging again. It also taught me how thoroughly wrong I had been to feel like an outsider before I was published.

DURING MY BOOK TOUR, I found communities of published and unpublished writers, and they each had voices and stories that were diverse, rich, beautifully done, and worthy of being heard. They were extraordinary in their work and their generosity of inclusion. They were there for each other, and now me.

That's where my reading series, Roar Shack, was born. I pushed myself past the idea that I wasn't good enough to belong and reached out to L.A. writers about starting a series. Any hesitancy I felt was outweighed by a desire to give writers a place to put themselves out there and be greeted in return by a community of creative, supportive, soon-to-be friends.

Through the series (now in its 5th year!) I hold the door

open the way a door was once held open for me. I try to foster a sense of community and belonging, because in the faces of writers who come to read or listen, I see that dawning realization that they've found a home.

Any doubt I still harbor about how far I've come is answered by my new novel, *The Night Language*, which was released on November 14, 2017. It tells the story of two young men thrown together by war. They're both outsiders who find themselves in the court of Queen Victoria. There they experience belonging and love before the inexorable tide of prejudice threatening to pull them apart.

Where my first novel depicted characters seeking their place in the world for the first true time, my second novel tells the story of characters finding that home, and fighting for the right to exist within it. My own arc, traceable through two novels. Not what I intended or planned, but right there for me, and now readers, to see.

Writing has been a teacher for me, and it's taught me this above all: Feeling like you don't belong simply means you haven't found where you belong yet. It's not a conclusion. It's an impetus, and as it turns out, life is never quite the same after you give yourself permission to belong.

17

LEARNING THE VALUE OF WRITING AS SELF-CARE

TERRI CONNELLAN

Writing 442,000 Words in the Most Challenging of Years

> *"We now structure our hours not to flee from fear, but to confront it and overcome it. We plan our activities in order to accomplish an aim. And we bring our will to bear so that we stick to this resolution."*
>
> – Steven Pressfield, Turning Pro

IT HAS TAKEN me a long time to realize the deep value of writing, especially when times are tough. Understanding that the act of writing is itself a guide and structure, a form of self-leadership in action, has been the biggest learning. It's not just a destination or product, something to tick off a list. It is a way of fortifying ourselves and our inner resources in times of change and in this, a form of self-care.

WRITING CAN FEEL like an extra thing to do, the one we never get to. It can feel like an indulgence or a luxury we will finally get to when we have carved out enough time, like a special piece of our heart waiting. We can put pressure on ourselves to create something, rather than seeing the process as the first step, the higher order piece of our lives that provides the framework for all the others.

I've had to learn through extreme life circumstances that writing can be a critical, stabilizing piece, a form of self-care that enables us to help others. The act of writing can feel selfish and self-indulgent, but it is often a life-saving, self-affirming act that provides quiet guidance. It strengthens us as we listen to our inner wisdom in whatever form of writing it chooses to take on: free writing, poetry, novel, journal or non-fiction book. These are all just different forms our voice can take to help us make sense of what is happening and to coalesce our experiences to say: Here I am, me, here in this world, now, here.

IT'S SAD that the harder life gets, the more chance there is that writing goes out the window as we struggle for time and attention, when it's exactly what we should do to brace ourselves as we move through winds of change.

I have just been through a period of massive transition. My mother was diagnosed with incurable metastatic breast cancer and I was her carer and close companion for over a year. Concurrently, my job was deleted after a successful thirty plus year career as a teacher and leader in the government adult education sector. I was made redundant, so my decision to choose to find another path as life coach and writer was overtaken by having to leave, with all the strange grief that this entails.

IN ALL OF THIS, writing was the central piece that I held on to as the core of my transition and reason for it. All my life I have wanted to be a writer, to express myself creatively and see my works out in the world in some way – as books, as blogs, as poems, as articles. It's been a key driver in my personal and work life. I've taught reading and writing for many years, taking that shadow career, as Steven Pressfield calls it, a long way as an underpinning structural piece to the writing I really wanted to do. And I've written more and every day, as the authentic heart of this journey.

I've realized if I don't write, the whole journey is meaningless.

So, I've had to shift my mindset about writing. Rather than seeing it as a task to be done, I now see writing as a necessary support at this time of change. I know that if I don't write, I can't make sense of what is occurring. I've had to seek ways to make writing the core of my days, breaking down the barriers and putting steps in to make sure it happens, like making time for daily exercise. Writing is a metaphor and reason, a tool to connect with my own feelings and strengths and to share them with others. I now see writing as a central self-leadership tool, a process in and of itself in the journey.

I wrote during this uncertain period, day in and day out, at a time when others, including myself in the past, might have given up or reprioritized. Even when I felt guilty or wrong or had to fight for it on a daily basis, I made writing the heart of this wholehearted journey. And I have found, reflecting back, that I have created volumes of words, my heart building and strengthening through a myriad of raw materials into blocks of writing over this time.

Through this cumulative process, I reinforced myself through the quiet act of writing. Each word, laid line by line, brick by brick, became a strengthening force, a buttress within the wall of myself. I shored up my self-belief and solidity, able to more strongly withstand whatever forces were thrown at me. That self-guiding support, created through words, settled and grounded me. Crafted over time, the words became a structure of their own, a cathedral of the imagination. So, I was both shaper and shaped, leaning into the unknown and moulded by it through writing.

A pivotal practice through this transition time was the daily edifice of getting back to Morning Pages, made famous by Julia Cameron. This practice kept coming to me in different ways around self-care. I saw that people who wrote Morning Pages also did other impressive creative work. So, on July 10 last year I started this practice and wrote day in day out, not missing too many days in a very chaotic time. I usually write three pages first thing in the morning on whatever it needs to be – stream of consciousness, what is worrying me, what I want to get done that day, what is blocking me, the challenges of the time.

Here are some words from that first entry on 10 July:

"So, this is the missing piece I am putting back. The central core. Me,

solitude, a pen, a piece of paper, quiet time, quiet writing as the authentic heart of me and all that I do. It's the simplest thing really. So why is it so hard? This action – pen moving across a white page is the closest thing to calm, authenticity, my voice, my thoughts, my feelings, I can get."

I HAVE WRITTEN around 184,000 Morning Pages words from July through to now, the volume of words reflecting the immense pain of grief and loss, including supporting my mother through terminal illness and the final stages of dying. Each written word was a brick placed in a framework that supported me. Through this, I strengthened the sense of being the architect of my life, reinforcing myself, directing what I could manage, which was the placement of one word at a time as a bulwark in the face of constant uncertainty.

The second writing practice was focused around tarot and intuition. A key goal in my transition has been to sharpen my intuitive practice through working with tarot and oracle. Over time, I developed a daily practice of tarot and oracle reading and writing intuitive guidance. From June to December in 2017, I created Tarot Narratives on social media, writing over 47,000 words of tarot-inspired guidance shared via an image in an intuitive still-life. I've shifted now to weekly deep-dive Tarot Narrative readings on my Quiet Writing blog, writing another 12,700 words this year.

THROUGH THIS PROCESS, I've honed the art of intuitive writing and working with tarot and oracle cards as a source of inner wisdom. I've learnt to work with the cycles of the moon and understand the yin and yang of that rhythm. Working with spirit and the energy of this time helped me tune into myself, another dimension of self-leadership. The gifts of tarot and links with writing have been profound and wise, guiding me and holding my hand, bolstering me through this time.

THE THIRD WRITING practice I've focused on is blogging. I've blogged for nearly eight years, but this past year has marked a return to consistent blogging, week in and week out. In September 2016, I relaunched Quiet Writing as my new blog and business.

Blogging has always been important to me as a way to hone my voice, to find out what I want to say and share in a more public way. I find it the most creative of acts, shaping a thought, inspiring resource, or intuitive reading into a blog post to share with others. Each piece is its own creative non-fiction piece, like a textured essay, weaving and connecting ideas.

OVER THE PAST 12 MONTHS, I have written 57 posts on a variety of topics including coaching, writing, reading, productivity, joy, introversion, personality, transition and intuitive tarot work. With about 97,000 original words, I've crafted and built my blog as I have reshaped and reinforced my life. I've shared my experiences of grief and loss, change and resilience, and my evolving resources for sustaining myself to in turn encourage and support others.

I've also sought out guest blogging opportunities, writing for other blogs and publications, focused on personality type and human resources. I've extended my leadership skills into a focus on self-leadership through becoming a life coach and gaining certification in Jung/Myers-Briggs personality type assessment. Writing about personality is a way to support my emerging, self-sustaining creative career and take my skills forward. It's a bridge spanning and augmenting my body of work over time, connecting it with more recent skill and knowledge development.

Based on personal experience, I've written about: learning to live the values of introversion; extraverted and introverted intuition; introversion and recruitment; leadership as self-leadership; and what neuroscience and neurodiversity can teach us about cognitive diversity in the workplace. I've also written a piece for the *inspired COACH Magazine* on books for emerging coaches.

IN ALL, I have written just over 12,000 words for guest blogging and feature article pieces, writing that required intensive background research and reading. This empowered me to flex my writing muscles into emerging areas and find my voice and unique zones of excellence. I can see how themes connect and my new practices relate to and build on previous experience.

Another key piece in the past year was writing my first e-book. I wanted this to be a substantial piece. Over many months, I revisited the key books that influenced my life and wrote *36 Books that Shaped my Story: Reading as Creative Influence*, in homage to my reading legacy.

At nearly 24,000 words and 94 pages, the experience of writing this book enabled me to step back and honour the inputs into my writing and life. In the repeated genres and reading experiences, I found insights I hadn't connected that I could take forward to write a new story at this time of change. Through this process, I learnt to write longer non-fiction creative pieces, to work with Scrivener writing software and to set up processes for sharing my work through my blog and email list, all critical to sharing my voice in the world. These tangible pieces of infrastructure were the practical skills for crafting my imagination into something more solid.

AND AS I headed towards November, it seemed that I might even step up to do NaNoWriMo, National Novel Writing Month, and attempt writing 50,000 words in a month. It was something I'd planned to do many times but hadn't followed through on. This year, I found that I was surprisingly well-placed to do this work. I had the outline of a non-fiction book entitled, *Wholehearted: Self-leadership for Women in Transition*. It wasn't a novel, but it was what I needed to write. I had just over 19,000 words written in the draft and the thorough outline showed me where I needed to go.

I had also prepared over time. It takes a village and a ton of groundwork to write a book. But I found I had prepared, piece by piece, via skilling up, showing up, seeking out individual and group coaching on my writing, reading blogs and listening to podcasts for many years such as Joanna Penn's fabulous *The Creative Penn* podcast. It was if it all coalesced into this moment of bringing my writing process and practice forward into something more substantial. As Steven Pressfield reminds us in *Turning Pro*, it's all about mindset shift and choosing to structure our hours, plan our days and turn up to do the writing.

I LEARNT that I could write 1,667 words a day in under an hour, breaking it up into two shorter chunks on a busy day.

Stretching myself, I wrote in many places: at home at my desk, in noisy cafes, in a plane, in hospital and in an airport departure lounge at the end of a full-on day. The Tide Pomodoro App became a close friend as I sought the peace and gentle routine it provided. And I watched my draft build as I consistently wrote around 1,667 words each day. By the end of November, I hit the 50,000-word target and became a NaNoWriMo winner, also reaching 69,346 words for my *Wholehearted* manuscript. I've added to it since and have nearly completed the first draft with a total of 78,088 words currently.

SADLY, my mother's condition started to deteriorate rapidly towards the end of November also. In hospital from late November, she did not return home, passing away on Christmas Day. This was the toughest experience in every respect, and trying to finish the last few thousand of my 50,000 words seemed so trivial and self-indulgent. But my journey of caring for my mother was also a journey in self-care, learning that looking after myself and meeting my critical needs was also a way of caring for my mother and her needs. In fact, it was dependent on it.

I managed to finish those words. I felt like a marathon runner crawling over the line at the end and the words weren't great. But those quiet times of sitting in the hospital cafe and other random spots, writing in snatched moments when emotionally exhausted, spoke to me of my commitment: writing as self-care and affirming practices for bringing my voice to bear in the world, however I could, in a year of complete upheaval, transformation and change.

. . .

So, I wrote it anyway or wrote it because writing is the ultimate act of self-care. These words were like the pieces of a cathedral I was building each day, shaping and buttressing myself through the act of writing. In the end, these words are the metrics of a year when hard, reinforcing, inner work was vital to my survival. They were the building blocks that structured my days, enabling me to be strong enough to support others. In all, from the practices mentioned in this essay, there are over 442,000 words writing a new life. And I can't imagine getting there in any other way than through the precious light of words aligned and the peace crafted from the moments of making them happen.

18

SOMETHING I COULDN'T YET HAVE

CAROLINE DONAHUE

The phone rang, a loud vibrating clang that echoed in the tiled hallway outside my bedroom. I stood in the doorway, uncertain whether or not I should pick up. Eventually, on the third ring, curiosity won out and I answered. It was a mistake. On the other end of the line the nasal voice began again with the list of questions I didn't want to answer. What was I doing, what music was I listening to, where was I in the room.

LATER, when I knew I had to report the phone calls to my teachers, I couldn't figure out how to communicate what it was specifically that made them so uncomfortable for me. I still can't say what it was that made me give him my number, what made it so scary to hang up the phone when I wanted to go. But I do know that the fear of that voice and what he later wrote about me shut off my writing voice for over twenty years.

Let's go back to the beginning.

When I was little, under six for certain, I developed book fever. Not just reading books either, but writing them, illustrating them, and attempting to publish them. I folded stacks of paper in half, inserted the pages into construction paper covers, and decorated the outside with a title, author name, and attempted to execute a full color design as well before stapling the booklets down the spine to complete my books. I did this over and over. We ran out of paper. My mother asked if I might want to write inside the books I had made already. I did write a treatise on bears that included the wise line, "every animal has its own scary way." Mostly, I kept making more and more blank books.

My family took notice and was incredibly supportive. At school, I was allowed to join every writing group that was offered and even went to a creative writing camp one summer. I have no recollection of anyone ever telling me it was a bad idea to write.

BUT THEN HIGH SCHOOL BEGAN. When I was about 16, I joined a creative writing class. I was thrilled. Finally, I could begin the process of becoming a real writer.

Until one of my creative writing classmates started calling me at night and asking all sorts of questions I didn't want to answer. During these conversations, I had no idea how to set boundaries. I wasn't prepared to say "no, I don't want to talk to you" or "I don't have to answer that question."

He asked me about music I liked and movies I enjoyed and, despite my discomfort, I answered his questions. They were straightforward enough, but there was something invasive about the way he asked them. The way his voice came through the phone like a snake. The way I felt cold when he spoke. The way I wanted to take a shower after we hung up. I didn't know how to say I had to go and that I didn't want to talk to him.

After all, I needed to be polite, right? Being a woman is about making other people feel comfortable, isn't it? For all the strong messages I received from my school and my family about what women are allowed to do, we weren't nearly so well briefed on all the things we don't have to do. They were so busy telling us that we could run the world now that they forgot to tell us how to tell someone to fuck off, thank you very much.

PARTWAY THROUGH THE SEMESTER, we began reading our work aloud. The only piece I remember was his.

He was pale, thin, and wore all black with round wire-rimmed glasses. I don't remember what color his eyes were, but in my mind they are as pale and eerie as his voice. He crossed his legs, one black lace-up booted foot hooked over his knee, and began to read.

In his story, a man was talking to a woman, but the story unfurled inside his head. As the character listened to the woman, he pictured her violently dismembered. He ripped her arms off, bit by bit, he took her apart and then dropped the pieces into a river. She kept talking, unaware of his fantasy. And then, at the end, the lyrics of a song floated into his mind. The lyrics of a song I had told him was my favorite.

I sat listening to him read and went cold all the way through my body. As soon as he set his paper down, I burst out of the room and hid in the student lounge, shaking. I flashed back to every phone conversation we had had, picturing him imagining me torn apart over and over. I felt sick.

In the coming weeks, I spoke to the dean of students, and I started hanging up the phone when he called. They told me nothing could be done unless I told him not to call me. The rules had to be followed. I had to say no before the school could step in. I spoke up, but I was still scared. I stayed away from class for a few sessions, but eventually I returned. I toughed it out.

As I finished high school and began college, I thought I had wiped this experience from my head. But as I turned 40 and wondered why I hadn't been able to finish all the novels I had begun this memory resurfaced.

Some things about my life have never added up when I have tried to understand them:

Despite the fact that I have told myself and others that I wanted to be a writer ever since I was stapling booklets together, I haven't been able to finish the manuscripts I've spent years and years writing.

I went to Kenyon College for my BA and, despite its having one of the best Creative Writing programs in the US, it never even occurred to me to take a class, let alone major in writing. It simply didn't occur to me at the time. Despite the fact that at one point John Green lived across the hall from me, for example. But then again, he wasn't "that John Green" yet.

. . .

I worked as an editor for an auction house and successfully took their catalogue from concept to print three times a year for three years with no hitches, yet when I started to think about publishing my own work in my 30s, I went into a cold sweat and decided the idea for the current novel I was working on wasn't viable and discarded it. Over and over again.

I have done NaNoWriMo to completion five times, and discarded my novel every single time.

This was never something I could explain. I took courses, got positive feedback from classmates and instructors, and put in time and effort to write stories and novels over and over, but I see now that the cold voice on the phone has been trying for decades to shut me down.

Even though all my teachers and my entire family supported my becoming a writer, my nervous system had decided that it wasn't safe.

"If you publish a book," his voice says, "I'll come back and this time I really will tear you apart."

Better to be a frustrated writer than dead. Even with an MA in Psychology, this message was buried so deep I didn't even know it was there. I just kept telling myself and everyone else that as soon as my schedule opened up a bit, I was going to crack down and finish that book.

And then in 2012, something happened. I was no longer satisfied by publishing an auction catalogue full of other people's writing. During the slow season, I started a blog called "The Book Dr." and wrote posts suggesting books in response to people's letters. I suggested books to go along with vacations, or books that would help people in tough situations.

I hit publish on post after post, and the site grew. I started dreaming about coaching and using my psychology skills again. I started working with writers and launched a podcast to interview other writers about how they had published their own books.

My writing self was beginning to fight back.

ON MY HONEYMOON IN 2016, I got an idea for a novel. Headed into the loo at Hops + Barley, a pub in Fredrichshain in Berlin, the plot exploded into my head. This book wasn't going to let me throw it in the garbage..

All those other manuscripts yelled at me from the drawer. "Are you going to ditch this book, like you've cut and run from all of us? Are you really going to write this book? Really?"

I HAD SOMETHING TO PROVE. I sat down with a notebook. I wrote scene after scene until I tangled myself up in knots. I needed to get clear on the story. I stepped back and made an outline, something I had never done before. It felt good. I felt the story snap into focus and with each day, I got to know my characters better. I understood who they were and why they did what they did.

The book became bigger than me.

As I write now, I often feel the shadow of that spidery voice hovering in the corners of my space. I can feel myself at sixteen scared and shaking in the student lounge. I see her holding the phone in my room, not knowing how to hang up.

But she's not in charge anymore. I am.

And I'll be damned if I let some self-obsessed teenage boy decide whether or not I get to write a novel. This isn't his book. This is my book.

I am writing this novel anyway. Even if it's terrible, even if people hate it – especially if it's terrible and people hate it.

I am writing this novel because I can. Because my life depends on it. And most of all, I am writing this book because I want my 16-year-old self to see that publishing this book will not kill me. It will not leave me mangled in parts in the bottom of the river.

Sometimes you have to do the thing that scares you the most to be set free. Please know that every day you sit down to write, every part of you that has been too scared to do it gets less scared and feels stronger.

Don't let your fears shut you down.

Write it anyway.

19

I SEE YOU, FEAR

JAZMINE ALUMA

I've always been full of ideas. I've dreamt up too many Etsy shops, coffee houses, magazines, crafts, and stories to count.

But if you know me, you know that I do not have an Etsy shop. Nor do I run a coffee house or a magazine. Despite being a multi-passionate idea machine, allowing those ideas to have wings of their own and live outside of my head has been my greatest creative challenge.

Two things pop up whenever an idea gets my blood pumping. First, I start talking it up, journaling about it, researching it, and then BOOM. Self-doubt.

SELF-DOUBT CAN BE such a cozy place to hang out. Right when I'm all fired up and about to take action, I think, *It will probably never work anyway*, or *It will suck*, or *It's far beyond my means*, or whatever. I think all these things to myself and then I think about going to get gelato.

And getting gelato seems a heck of a lot nicer than starting something that's bound to fail. So, I figure I might as well forget about it and focus on more attainable goals like, getting to the gelato shop before it closes. And that idea of mine? Well, there will be other, better, more attainable ideas. I'll just sit and eat my stracciatella while I wait for those ideas to find me.

But, let's just say I've conquered my self-doubt and I'm ready to do something exciting, to follow my passion. Then comes the next hurdle. BOOM. Fear. Now I've got a whole different issue to deal with.

Oh, fear. You're such an a-hole.

As if overcoming my self-doubts wasn't hard enough. Now I have to look fear in the face and say, *Screw you?* Most of the time, I'd rather not.

ONE PASSION of mine that has outlived all fly-by-night ideas is pen and paper. The written word is like the embrace of a parent; it's the thing I run both toward and from depending on what's going on inside.

I started blogging several years ago. I didn't know what I was doing. I just got on the computer and wrote stuff. Then I'd get distracted or lose interest and shut the site down. After a bit, I'd see what other people were doing on their blogs, get inspired and start another one. And so on. Like a dysfunctional romance, it became a pattern of love and unlove – something inside of me lighting up and then flickering at the slightest of gusts.

That "gust" is fear. It's the thing that makes me abandon blogging (or any writing endeavor for that matter). Every single time.

. . .

A FEW FEARS that have stopped me cold in the past:
- What if *no one* reads what I write?
- What if no one cares?
- What if *someone* reads what I write?
- What if I offend someone?
- What if they send me hate mail?
- What if I write something so preposterous that it is shared on social media just so people can laugh at me?
- What if I write and write and write and it never gets me anywhere?
- What if...?

IN 2014 MY son was born. Motherhood completely derailed me. After a year of sleep deprivation, diapers, and breastfeeding I was ready to get back to the page. Like, super ready. Like itchy, get-out-of-my-way-'cause-I've-got-something-to-say ready.

Did fear stop me? Yeah. It totally did. It stopped me, and then I looked right at it and kept going.

FEAR USUALLY LEAVES ME PARALYZED. Frozen in my path. Abandoning ship. Like many times in the past, I could have just sat down and ditched the thing I wanted most. But I didn't.

This time I was more fearful of what would happen if I *stopped*.

Instead of ticking off all the "what-ifs" that might happen if I kept writing, I looked at the what-ifs that might happen if I *didn't*. And they were a hell of a lot worse than any imagined hate-mail.

- *What if my son finds my writing someday and asks me why I stopped?*

- *What if I tell him to follow his passions and he asks me why I quit mine?*
- *What if I make up excuses like,* I was busy taking care of you?
- *What if he tells me I should have kept writing?*

Ouch.

The thought of being a failure in my son's eyes is so much scarier than anything I could possibly imagine. So, I keep on writing.

I keep on writing because it would be harder to stop than to continue.

REALIZING this has forced me to look right at fear, to completely acknowledge it, to even entertain it. I believe that when we are really honest with ourselves about our fears, we can use them as fuel for following our passions. We have to see what we're scared of and then find what we're even *more* scared of. We'll get nowhere in life by avoiding fear. The only way to move past it is to look at it, walk into it, and acknowledge every dark corner of it. We have to *go there* before we can get anywhere.

20

YOUR KNOCKBACKS PROPELLED ME FORWARDS

VALERIE GRIFFIN

Writing is subjective. We all have our own unique style and we all have our own reasons for writing. The world is full of stories and the diversity is finite. There is something for every preference be it genre, point of view, plot driven or character driven.

I have doubts all the time with my writing. I often edit to within an inch of insanity. I have to make myself let it go and submit, put myself on show to the world. But I love it when, now and again, you just know that this is the piece - the piece that makes it all worthwhile.

I RECENTLY ENROLLED on a six week online creative writing taster course. We had to write a short story, upload it and then we all had to practice the art of critiquing three random pieces of work. The criteria was, that for every negative comment, there had to be a positive (there is always a positive) and that all the comments had to be constructive (us writers can be fragile creatures and prone to insecurities). Personally, I don't need to receive unwarranted negativity, I can do that for myself about my writing, thank you very much. So to all you people out there who want to burden us with negativity…don't. Show us some encouragement instead.

The main thing is, if writing makes us happy, then that's all that matters. I write because I have to. It's not a choice. It's something I need to do to otherwise I get scratchy and grumpy (even more than usual!).

I FIRST STARTED WRITING over twenty-five years ago then stopped because life stepped in and I started again five years ago. Back then there was no internet so I joined a postal writing group. Basically, when the parcel arrived we read everyone's stories, commented on them in the enclosed notebook, added a new story of our own and posted it off to the next person. As always, there was one person who always gave me a negative review and was often scathing in his comments. I wondered was it because I was much younger, or was it because I was the only member of the group that had been published and he was jealous. Thankfully, being much younger I was filled with the resilience and confidence only youth can give you. I decided to enclose a copy of a short story that had been runner-up in a competition, but I didn't tell them this. When the parcel came back to me I left his comment until last and read the others, all of which were positive. His comments, however, were a vitriolic damnation of my piece, saying it was a predictable load of rubbish with a typical, well-worn theme.

NOW TODAY, I would still seethe and be angry and probably

want revenge at his nastiness, but I would leave it, be the better person. But back then, I couldn't let it pass. I reviewed all the stories, even his, and gave my reviews then I wrote a message just for him, in the notebook. I wrote that my predictable load of rubbish had been awarded runner-up in a writing magazine's competition and that he was a blinkered, bitter and jealous man and I resigned from the group, which was a shame.

A COUPLE of years ago I wrote a short story based on a prompt from my writing group. The story then gave me the idea for a novel. When I read the story out to the group, I received constructive feedback. I let the idea roll around in my head for a while then decided I needed guidance on how to start, so I booked myself on a course. I submitted the story to the tutor to showcase my writing. It was slammed. 'What is this?' asked the tutor. 'Why have you given me this?'

I explained about it triggering the idea for a novel.

'Well, where's the novel?'

'I don't have the novel yet,' I replied. *Excuse me!! That's why I'm here on this novel writing course!* I felt like packing up and going home. I'd come to learn, to receive something constructive to work on, not someone waving a piece of A4 at me.

But I still keep writing. I have a great support network around me, writers and authors who encourage me, who offer constructive guidance and advice. And over the past year I have had quite a few pieces published, so thank you all.

In November 2017 I drafted out 65,000 words during NaNoWriMo and now, one year on, I'm on my third draft.

The short story that triggered it all is below. See...I'm writing it anyway!

Not a Good Year for Runner Beans

At 6.08am on 14 April 1942, Jack Humphries was woken by the sound of the cows lowing. He frowned. Alfie should be milking them by now. Careful not to wake his wife, he slid out of bed and pulled his faded overalls on over his nightshirt. He put his head round the door of Alfie's room. The bed hadn't been slept in. He went downstairs to the kitchen. On the pine table, propped between the salt cellar and the sugar bowl, was a handwritten note. Jack screwed it up. He didn't need to read it. He walked out of the kitchen and across the yard to the barn.

As soon as he arrived on the farm that morning, Billy knew from Jack's face that Alfie had done what he'd been threatening.

"Did you know?" asked Jack. Billy lowered his eyes. He couldn't lie. Jack sighed.

"Well, we'd best we get on. The farm won't run itself."

Over the next few months Jack and Billy, with the help of the Women's Land Army, ploughed the fields and planted and harvested crops.

BARELY SIX MONTHS after Alfie's departure, Jack was in the top field harvesting carrots, the throaty chug of the tractor drowning out the land girls' chatter. Straightening up, he put his arthritic hands into the small of his back and stretched backwards. Looking out over the farm, he saw a lone cyclist navigating the rutted track leading to the farmhouse. Raising his hands to block out the early afternoon sun, Jack recognised Jimmy Mackinson. Cold fingers gripped and squeezed his heart, causing his breath to escape in an anguished groan. Jimmy and Alfie were best mates and, under normal circumstances, Jack would have welcomed him. But not today. Having been asthmatic from childhood, Jimmy's role in the war was different to Alfie's. You didn't want him knocking on your door when he was in uniform.

He watched helplessly as the angel of death dismounted, leant his bike against the wall and approached the weathered farmhouse door. Jack held his breath, waiting for his wife to open it. Did he hear her scream or did he just imagine it? He couldn't say. He watched as she took the telegram from Jimmy and slumped against the door frame. He watched as Jimmy bowed his head and backed away. Despite his own loss, Jack's heart went out to the lad, to his courage.

As the days shortened, the war lengthened. The cows bellowed often, reminding Jack he was late with the milking. Every day, he slouched back and forth across the courtyard, his worn boots scuffing the rough concrete, each step heavy with raw emotion and tiredness. Each time, he passed the kitchen garden without a glance. The runner beans, planted by Alfie the day before he left, hung neglected on their makeshift frames, the full pods brittle and browned, the leaves skeletal and crumbling. They were too painful a reminder of the loss and grief a father should never have to feel.

21

TRAVELING THROUGH A FIRST DRAFT WITH THE FOOL

KIM MANGANELLI

"In the beginner's mind there are many possibilities, but in the expert's there are few."
~ Shunryu Suzuki

Over the past two and a half years of writing my current novel, I have discovered that there are two crucial ingredients to creating a first draft: time and a willingness to play the Fool. Writing groups and handbooks can be helpful, as can Scrivener, a vintage typewriter, or even a vision board with an image of Oprah with her arms outstretched to you and your yet-to-be-written book. But when it comes to sitting down and just getting the words on the page for a first draft, you need time and you need to be a Fool.

As a tenured professor of nineteenth-century literature and a mom of a curious two-year-old, time can be a scarce resource, especially when you add in the unexpected doctor's visits, daycare plagues, and sleep regressions that can result in missed days of work and sleepless nights. But time can be found in the cracks and corners of just about any day. I've whipped out my notebook and written in my car before heading into faculty meetings. I've written whole scenes in my head in the shower and then recorded the details in the Notes app on my phone while sitting on the edge of the tub. Many afternoons, I manage to write for 15 to 20 minutes before I pick up my son from daycare at 4:30. Although it often feels impossible, time can be found if I want to find it badly enough. Conversely, if I want to feel like there is no time because I'm overwhelmed by all the admin and grading for my day job, all the laundry that needs folding, and all the closets and cabinets that need to be KonMaried, I can look at my day or week ahead and see that there's absolutely no time to be found.

. . .

I've come to understand that my personal relationship to time really comes down to my state of mind. When I was on maternity leave, I paid for the time to write by hiring a babysitter to come for two to three hours in the afternoon a few days a week so I could get some words on the page. And you better believe that when I was paying $13 an hour for writing time, the choice became clear: am I going to use this time to work on my novel or am I going to scroll to the end of the internet? Once I was writing a check for it each week, missing out on time with my baby to scroll to the end of the internet was much less desirable.

This past year, I learned that it also takes time to figure out what story I'm telling. Although the characters for my novel began to emerge in my imagination in November 2015 (thanks to a fortuitous viewing of *The Man from U.N.C.L.E.* Thank you, Guy Ritchie!), it took me almost two years to figure out the narrative I wanted to write about them. The idea for how to tell a story about these characters first flashed into my mind in January 2016, but after a month or two of trying to write it, I became overwhelmed and scared and decided to toss that idea aside for something "easier," something that felt more doable, an idea that would allow me to crank out a fast and dirty draft in less than a year. (Oprah is waiting, after all!). After spinning my wheels and trying out "easier" narratives through the first half of 2016, I finally cried "uncle" (sorry, I couldn't help it) and came back to the plot that still makes me jittery with both excitement and anxiety when I think about it. When I recommitted to my original idea in July 2016 on a cloudy afternoon while I was tucked safely into my bed with my writing notebook open on my lap and my two kitties sleeping beside me, I felt like I was walking right off a cliff.

ENTER THE FOOL. Writing the first draft of this novel has taught me to embrace the first card in tarot's Major Arcana. In the traditional Rider Waite Smith tarot deck, the Fool card features a guy in happy yellow boots staring up at the sky as the sun warms his back. He's holding a white flower in one hand, a small knapsack hangs over his shoulder, and a playful white dog jumps about his heels as he cheerfully walks toward the edge of cliff. The Fool is the card of infinite possibilities, stepping into the unknown, and new beginnings. Even though the dog, a symbol of being tamed and domesticity, seems to be trying to warn him that he's right at the edge, the Fool is going to follow his true heart's desire wherever it takes him. He perfectly embodies what it feels like to fully commit to writing a first draft of a novel. In fact, since the Fool is the Zero card in the deck, it might be more accurate to describe the very first draft of a novel as a discovery draft or a "zero draft," a concept I learned many years ago from reading Joan Bolker's bible for all graduate students, *How to Write Your Dissertation in Fifteen Minutes a Day*. The "zero draft" is all of the brainstorming and series of trial and error experiments that come before a first draft can be written. This initial draft can be a collection of notes, a detailed outline of possibilities, or a series of freewrites from which first draft material is then extracted. Without realizing it, all of the notes and scenes that I wrote between November 2015 and July 2016 were essentially my zero draft for this novel.

Now that I have figured out what story I'm telling, I would love to move into a more knowing card in my tarot deck. How fantastic would it be to feel like the Empress each and every day I sit down to write? For me, the Empress is the Beyoncé card in any deck. She has mastered her craft, she knows how to inhabit this world as a woman, artist, and mother, and she is comfortable in her own skin. My favorite representation of her is in the *Wild Unknown* deck in which she is a white tree whose branches are edged in fuchsia flames as a crescent moon rises in the black sky above. She is a fecund figure who represents abundance, creativity, and fertility. She is essentially a summer day when all is ripe and right in the world. At some point, perhaps once my current novel has been through many rounds of revision and has made its way out into the world, I may wake up feeling like The Empress. (I have a feeling I will need to write four or five novels before I truly feel like I'm inhabiting the spirit of this card). But for now, the first draft of this novel is best served by my playing the Fool.

EVEN THOUGH I know that playing the Fool is what the first draft of my novel most needs from me right now, it is difficult to slip into this mindset. This is no surprise given all of my academic training and my day job as a professor of literature. While the Fool carries a little knapsack that's only big enough for a pocket Moleskine, a couple of pens, a tarot deck, and maybe a couple of granola bars, I'm lugging behind me steamer trunks filled with the literature and scholarship that I've spent the past 20 years "mastering" as a teacher and scholar of nineteenth-century British and American literature. Both my greatest asset and obstacle as a writer is that I have built a career learning and teaching others how to take apart great works of literature.

When my sliver of writing time opens up, it can be

hard to shift out of the mindset of the literary expert I've been trained to be. There's a comfort and assurance, indeed a certainty, that comes with expertise, which can be a great asset to possess in the revision and editing stages of a writing project. But as Toni Morrison said in her 1993 *Paris Review* interview, "Schools are only important to me when I'm teaching literature. It doesn't mean anything to me when I'm sitting here with a big pile of blank yellow paper." Although it feels sacrilegious to place Toni Morrison and "Fool" in the same sentence, she has built a career out of knowing how to play, experiment, and take chances on the page.

BUT EVEN WHEN I set aside my steamer trunks filled with the words of Austen, the Brontës, George Eliot, Faulkner, and of course, Toni Morrison, just to name a few, my reality does not match that of the Fool's. I have chosen for my journey to be a family road trip rather than a solo venture. My version of the Fool's journey includes a mini-SUV filled with my husband, toddler, and aging parents, not to mention my 40 students each semester and all of the papers and projects I've asked them to produce for my classes.

Even when I'm physically alone, I've still got plenty of voices in my head that I sometimes have to twirl on as I write. I have the booming voices of the big dreamers who are already bouncing around to "Big Pimpin'" as they dream of meeting Oprah and giving readings at the bookstores in all my favorite cities (never mind that I'm still writing my way through a first draft). Then there's the chorus of literary critics who like to call out the clichés and banal plot points and other forms of "bad" writing, and who live for footnoting all of the various literary influences

I'm gleaning from other writers before I can even punctuate the sentence I've written.

And then there are the siren songs of the "live your best life," "follow your purpose," and "jump and the net will catch you" voices who want to ditch the mini-SUV to start a new life with my husband and little one in New Orleans as a novelist and novice tarot reader, hurricanes and housing costs be damned.

The seven tips below are helping me to manage my time and my mind on my Fool's journey toward completing a first draft.

Rules of the Road for Traveling with the Fool

If you're familiar with the Fool, you already know that rules are not really her thing. She's all about that path less traveled—the more brambles and winding unpaved paths, the better. But even the most adventurous traveler needs to consult a map or at the very least check in with locals about the best places to eat, sleep, and those hidden gems that aren't going to be found in the most thorough guidebooks. So, here are seven guide posts that can help you travel with the Fool as you write your first draft.

1. **You don't have to write every day.** I know this sentence may make some of you clutch your pearls (or perhaps your gold chains) while you say Mr. T style, "I pity the Fool." But if you don't believe me, check out these words of wisdom from a recent *Author's Guild* interview with Tayari Jones, author of 4 novels, whose most recent book, *An American Marriage*, was selected for Oprah's Book Club: "When we tell people that they must write every day, it makes

people who work, people who perform childcare, eldercare, people who have other responsibilities think, 'Oh, I can never be a writer.' It makes people feel that writing is for a privileged class of people who, if they weren't writing, would be eating bonbons." Jones expands on this wisdom in a Rutgers University at Newark interview when she says, "Even if you don't write every day, if you write often, you will get your book done. So many important stories are in the hearts and minds of very busy people." If you're still not convinced, then perhaps the words of Toni Morrison from a 1978 interview will persuade you. She was working as a Senior Editor at Random House, teaching at Yale, and raising her two sons on her own when she offered the following insight into her writing life: "I don't write every day. I only think about it every day. But I think one thing that happens is that you learn to use time for more than one thing….When I'm writing a book, there's almost no time when it's not on my mind—when I'm driving, doing dishes, or what have you. So by the time I get to the manuscript page, I have had some very clear thoughts about what I want to do!" Just about any parent and any person with a full-time job, especially if that job is related to writing or teaching, will tell you that it is impossible to get words on the page or screen every single day. However, like Morrison, I do think about my characters and their lives every single day.

2. **When you do write, create a tiny road map for your scene and for your day.** You

don't have to outline the whole novel—that's the surest way to make any Fool lose interest and stake out new territory in a completely unrelated project. But maybe while you're making coffee, map out 2-3 sensory details or moments of action in your current or upcoming scene. This way your Fool can't wander off to explore tarot decks on Pinterest when you're supposed to be writing about your heroine showing up at a party in Savannah. Also, create a tiny road map for your day so that you have some idea of when and where you might write. Sometimes I stop at a park on my way to pick up my little one and write for 10 or 15 minutes in my car.

3. **Two crappy pages (or sentences) a day keep the gremlins away.** This crucial bit of wisdom came to me by way of Marie Forleo's interview with Tim Ferriss. Although Ferriss's reality does not match my own, I'm happy to take advice from anyone who has figured out how to create a 4-hour work week. Ferriss's writing advice has kept my novel alive during two hectic semesters. When you do write, give yourself a small doable goal that matches the reality of your day. During winter break, I managed to settle into a lovely steady rhythm of writing two pages a day, but when the new semester started and everyone in my house was stricken by a flu-like muppet plague in January, I missed a whole week of writing because two pages suddenly felt like too much. So, I told myself that if I could just write two sentences, that would be good enough. Currently, I'm able

to write at least a page 5 or 6 days a week, but on the really busy days or the days when one or more members of my household are sick or engaged in an epic tantrum, it's helpful to know that I can get down two sentences and then head back into the fray.

4. **Put good voices in your ears.** Dani Shapiro often shares the wisdom she learned from the poet Jane Kenyon who said, "Read good books, have good sentences in your ears." In addition to reading broadly, listening to podcasts is now a key component of my writing life. My favorite podcasts, such as Caroline Donahue's *The Secret Library*, Tiffany Han's *Raise Your Hand Say Yes*, Linda Sivertsen's *Beautiful Writer's Podcast*, and the two seasons of Elizabeth Gilbert's *Magic Lessons* show me how other writers and artists have traveled with their Fools. Sometimes I also search the podcast library to find individual episodes featuring my favorite authors and creators. My 45-minute commute to and from school allows me to sink into the lives of the guests featured on these podcasts and the very best episodes leave me yearning to get back to work on my novel.

5. **Apprentice yourself to someone**. My dear friend and colleague, Jillian Weise, gives her students this assignment in her poetry workshops, asking her students to pick a poet whose work they would like to learn from and perhaps emulate. Earlier this year, I found myself craving the words of Morrison like someone with a vitamin deficiency. Although the time hasn't opened up for me to sink into

the worlds within her novels, I have been reading her collected interviews while my little one plays. I am especially loving the early interviews before she was TONI MORRISON, Nobel Laureate (said in Oprah's booming voice) since she offers so many details and insights into how she conducted her writing life when she was a working mom. In addition to looking for writers who are writing the types of books you like to read, also look for writers who are living the kind of life you're living. I've gained so much wisdom from reading interviews featuring writers like Emma Straub and Jesmyn Ward, who are mothers to small children. I've also sought the wisdom of tenured academics like Deborah Harkness, Mary Bly (aka Eloisa James), and Viet Thanh Nguyen, who wrote novels on the side while pursuing their scholarly careers.

6. **Beware of the Heirophants.** In the tarot, the Heirophant is the all-knowing spiritual teacher and authority. He's an embodiment of orthodoxy and conformity. In the writing world, the Heirophants can often be found in the online programs and guidebooks of "experts" who offer to sell you the secret to writing your novel in a month or 90 days. Or they're the literary establishment who declare what a "good" or "marketable" novel is. As Roxane Gay said in her beautiful pep talk for 2017's NaNoWriMo, "This is your novel and only you know how to write it." By all means seek out inspiration, read and listen to interviews with your favorite writers, and buy a guidebook or

two if you think seeing them on your desk will remind you of your purpose. But no one can tell you how to write the first draft of your novel. Be willing to be a Fool and write it badly one sentence at a time. You will learn how to write your novel by writing all the way to the end of your first draft.

7. **Become a student again.** Find an area of your life in which you can play, learn, make a mess, and get it wrong. I know what you're thinking: "I don't even have time to write the thing I've been called to write, and you're seriously telling me to add another hobby to my list?!" Yes, that's what I'm telling you. To expand into a new area of interest, start by following people on Instagram and other social media platforms who are doing work you're curious about. Or, look to see if there are YouTube tutorials or maybe even an online class you could take. My current obsession with tarot has allowed me to become a novice again. I get to learn a whole new system of knowledge, and I get to study all of the different interpretations of the cards as I learn to formulate my own. Every single day I learn something new—whether it's about a new interpretation of a card I thought I knew well or perhaps a new tarot podcast, Instagram feed, or deck that I can't wait to get my hands on like Egan's southern-based tarot, *Delta Enduring*. With tarot, I am truly a student again. I can be curious, take notes, and wonder without worrying what the end product or result will be. The sole purpose of my study is for my own

giddy pleasure. With tarot, I can play the Fool guilt-free and without consequence, which in turn has been a great reminder to me for how I want to approach my writing sessions as I create the first draft of my novel.

———

Each day, I have to be willing to play the Fool when I sit down to continue writing my first draft. And each day, when I look at the books that line my shelves and that create haphazard towers that threaten to tumble across my desk, I have to remind myself that each of those authors survived their Fool's journey. They managed to navigate their external and/or internal obstacles, they twirled on their gremlins and haters, and saw their work through to publication.

For each book we write, we have to be willing to become the Fool again and again and again because we won't know how to write that next story, poem, novel, or memoir until we've written it. I wish you and your first drafts well on your Fool's journeys. As the French say, "Bon voyage et bonne chance!" And who knows, maybe one day several years from now, if you happen to visit New Orleans, you'll come across my candlelit table while you take a twilight stroll around Jackson Square. I'll be the card reader who is smiling to herself as a little white dog plays by her feet.

22

LIVE WIRE WRITER

MICHELLE AINSLIE

Writing helps me untangle surging strings of current in my brain. Each day, as I put words on the page, my anxiety unfurls and I can put thoughts into straight rows again and make sense of them. The less I write, the more tangled my thoughts become, and eventually knots of absolute panic form. I know that if I let it get to this point that life will truly become unmanageable.

It sounds exaggerated. It sounds extreme. But it's true. Writing keeps me sane. Writing keeps me alive. Ironically, however, on some days writing is the hardest thing in the world to do.

I WAS DIAGNOSED with bipolar disorder in 2015, but I have been living with it, unlabelled, my entire life. It makes being a writer exceptionally difficult, but on the other edge of the same sword, provides the fuel for fiery creativity.

Bipolar disorder is an illness of extremes. It creates a volatile world of paper cards. It can tower into something beautiful and just as easily come violently crashing down. It has stolen so many of my relationships, enormous amounts of money, and boxes and boxes of dreams. It has also given me creativity, opportunities and unwrapped surprises I would not have thought possible in my one tiny life.

Creating and managing my world as a writer has always had to be in the house that bipolar built. I have to work within the architecture I have been given, and some corners are really cramped, parts of the ceiling keep caving in, and other large spaces make me feel anxious and alone. But over time I have learnt to make it my own. I have made it home.

STARTING my own business had to fit into the wild and crazy. This meant adjusting my routine depending on where my mood is on the graph, knowing when to take a break before I am triggered, deciphering what the signs are and learning to work with them. I can't just decide I am going to write a book, set up a 6-month writing schedule, and then slot my work into a diary.

As a freelance copywriter I have deadlines, but as a *bipolar* copywriter I bleed into those lines and I know that if I meet a client's needs while I am depressed, it will inevitably mean that there will be a lot of sacrifice in coming weeks on a personal level. When I push myself too hard when I am down, I burn out very quickly. I get physically ill and need to cut out "real life" to give myself recovery time.

VERY FEW PEOPLE understand this need to reboot after a depressive cycle. Especially one where I was forced to work and function in order to keep my business afloat. It isn't easy to comprehend how much energy it takes to get that final document in on time, when quite honestly, I don't even have the means to get out of bed and brush my teeth. But still, I get my word count in. I have happy clients. And then I have to pay the price, which usually means the invoices I receive don't match.

When I'm manic, ideas flit and dance around me like miniature birds, and I just want to catch one for a brief moment, have a look at all its shiny colours, and then let it go again. Then catch the next, and the next. But while I'm jumping and running after tiny birds, the sentences start coming in through the windows and the doors and if I don't write them down they threaten to suffocate me in my own house. So I write until my stomach is knotted with the pressure of having to get every single word out before the muse consumes all the space. Then I see another bird, another idea, and I jump up, sentences still pouring in through every hole, demanding expression.

OF COURSE, much like if I were to write while drunk (Hemingway did this often, I have yet to try it), not much makes sense when I read over my work in a sane, sober state. Words trip over each other and fall into gutters that no editing can save. Every now and again there is a gem or two, but finding them is tedious. I spend much of my normal-mooded time sifting and sorting through reams of writing I penned while manic, hoping to find something coherent and useful, and if I am really lucky, beautiful.

WHEN I'M DEPRESSED there are no stories. There are no birds. The windows and doors are nailed shut and nothing comes inside. Sentences dry up like autumn leaves outside; the words that are meant to be mine are crunched under the boots of those who walk past. Parents. Doctors. Boyfriends. Even sometimes, unintentionally, I will hear a crack, lift my shoe, and go fuck…I just broke my own reputation again. By stepping in shitty words and calling it writing.

When I'm depressed it takes energy to get out of bed and go to the bathroom. It is a monumental decision-making process to make coffee. There is no motivation to live, and certainly no reason or inspiration to write. There are no words. There is no meaning. Nothing matters.

There is also the added weight of believing that I am not good enough. That everything I have ever written is terrible and I can't believe people actually buy my books or read my poems. I feel like a fraud that stepped into a world that isn't my own, dared to call myself a writer, and now, here I am – a complete fuck-up that can't even read the instructions on the packet of soup I want to make. The only thing left in the cupboard, of course, because when I'm depressed I don't leave the house and I certainly don't go shopping for food.

I stare at the ceiling, the walls, the floor. I stroke the cat absentmindedly. I waste hours. Days. When I manage to actually start the laptop, I may stare at the blank screen for hours. The challenge is to force myself to get one sentence out. Usually one will encourage another. I don't often write more than a paragraph, but if I try hard enough I know that a few sentences are actually possible. The beautiful irony is that if I manage to push past the pain and the exhaustion, the writing I do while I'm depressed is often the best work I produce.

. . .

So in true bipolar disorder fashion, my worst work is written when I have the most energy and ideas and believe with all my heart that I am brilliant. I write pages and pages and pages of the stuff. On the flip side, my best work is produced when writing is the last thing I want to do, when I think that every word I come up with is shit, and when I have no energy to produce anything more than a couple of sentences.

I can flit between hypomania and depression several times a week. One day I will be churning out tens of thousands of words that are pretty crap (even though I feel almighty), and the next I will battle to put together a single phrase (which I will vehemently believe is terrible). In my neutral moods in-between, which are rare, I use the time to edit and make something of the chaos I created.

But still…I write anyway.

Bipolar disorder, difficult as it is, comes tattooed with creativity. I have never seen one without the other. As a writer I owe much of my talent to the way my brain has been wired, including the bipolar electric highways. So although my illness makes writing incredibly difficult, it is also makes it possible.

And, as with most obstacles to writing and to life, success comes down to a choice. I could toss out all my ideas when I am manic, knowing that they will probably amount to nothing anyway, and go shopping instead. But I choose to sit down and write regardless because I also know that amongst all the nonsensical shit there will be pieces of a book, shards of a poem, something magical that I can use.

When I am depressed it would be much easier to sleep or eat my way through the pain and not write at all. But I write anyway. Because I have seen what happens when I force myself through.

WRITING IS BEAUTIFUL. Writing is art. Writing breathes. I would not want a life without words moving through me every day – through the books I read and the stories I write; flowing through the bones that hold me up and give me form.

Writing is the mould I shape my life into, and through it I have created a world where even having bipolar disorder turns out to be pretty damn fantastic.

23

DEAR MOM WHO WRITES

KALYANI DESHPANDE

Dear Mom Who Writes,

I HEREBY GIVE you the permission to leave your house on a Saturday afternoon and go write at Starbucks. As you back out of the driveway, you'll undoubtedly question your worth as a wife and mother. You'll wonder if your kids will hate you for leaving them (they won't); you'll worry whether your husband will give them a snack on time (he won't, but the kids will live); you'll ask yourself if you turned off the stove (you did); you'll cringe at having to fold three loads of laundry when you get back (plus the load in the dryer, which makes four).

As you pull into the Starbucks, you'll doubt your abilities as a writer. You haven't published anything yet. You haven't finished the novel you started two years ago. You have character sketches in Evernote, scenes outlined in the

Draft folder of your email, and dialogue scribbled on the many post-it notes that live in your purse. The last time you wrote on your blog was six months ago and you still have just five people on your mailing list (your mom, your aunt, your best friend, your sister, and your husband).

You locate a table near the window, put your bag down and take a seat. You run your hands through your hair – you can't believe you finally made it here. You open your laptop and see the dozen open tabs on your browser, articles you need to read for work. If you spend the next couple of hours working, you'll be "ahead of the game". You'll have a smarter-sounding update at the Monday morning meeting and your manager will finally give you that promotion he's been promising you since last year.

You close the laptop, feeling a little dizzy. The work, the unfinished novel, the kids – it all feels like too much.

You pull out your phone and get on Facebook. The author whose book you abandoned last week just got another book deal. The author you recently discovered writes in her office that overlooks a pond where ducks wade peacefully. The author whose prose makes you ache with awe is twenty-seven, has three New York Times bestsellers and flawless skin to boot.

Mom, relax. Put down the phone and take a deep breath. Walk up to the counter and order your coffee. Go ahead and indulge – get the whipped cream. Then, get your coffee, sit down and listen:

Your kids are safe – happy, even. There will always be laundry to fold – always. You'll get the work done – you somehow always do. Don't believe everything you see on social media.

Your kids need your novel. They need to know that you can follow your passion, while raising a family and working a full-time job. They need to know that what you love needs to be nurtured for it to grow. They need to see their mom set a goal and accomplish it.

Your work needs your novel. Your team needs to be inspired by someone who's happy not just at work, but in her life. Finishing your novel will give you the confidence to take on more challenging projects. You'll be more willing to step out of your comfort zone, knowing that only the very best of things are waiting for you there.

Your soul needs your novel. You need to honor the idea that chose you – *it* chose you, Mom. Yes, it makes absolutely no sense, but why then, does it cause that flutter in your stomach every time you think about it? Why, when you decide to give up on it, do you read something in the newspaper and think, *I should add that to the plot* or hear snatches of a conversation and think, *my character would say something like that.*

REMEMBER how it felt being nine years old, finishing one Nancy Drew book and diving joyfully into the next? Remember when your best friend in business school begged you to change your major to English because she was blown away by your essays and stories? Remember how you tore through novels by Chitra Divakaruni Banerjee, Arundhati Roy, Indu Sundaresan and Toni Morrison and thought, *what if I could write like that?* Remember when you sat down one day and started writing?

So now, take a deep breath and a long sip of your decadent, frothy, Caramel Macchiato. Open your laptop and write.

. . .

Signed,
A Mom Who Writes

24

RATTLER

TERI VELA

I love stories. I love reading them and writing them, hearing them and thinking through them. I love hypotheticals as possible story-lines, and matching known experiences with unknown elements, and turning it all over in my head.

As a child, I wanted to be a writer and I'm not sure where I got that from. No one in my family was a "professional" writer, and few have jobs in creative arts, but I had it in me, as a characteristic. A characteristic that I now understand as a relationship with divinity or spirituality because it is a larger understanding of the whole of me. I have always felt a driving curiosity with the written word.

As soon as I could read I barreled through books, and I felt real pride upon receiving my first dictionary. I was about eight and my mother gifted me a little pocket dictionary to stick in my backpack. She suggested words to look up, and I sat there in the food court of a mall going through the process. Paging through the small print to find the right one. We thought it was fun.

I am not sure if the dictionary present was a reaction to my preference for writing or from my parents' understanding of the English language, but either way it stuck with me. English was a second language for both my mother and my father, and this may explain the way they absorbed it. They studied it and admired it and passed that relationship down to me. When I was ten I wrote a poem in fancy cursive announcing that I hoped to be a writer.

YET TWENTY PLUS YEARS LATER, here I am, not living as a "professional writer". I am a lawyer, which is not a bad job, and I realize I am fortunate to be able to write that. I research and write as a part of my job, and this is also fortunate.

Fortune though, often feels relative. I keep writing close to me in other ways, with reading and podcasts about writing, and by walking around with two or three journals on me at all times, but something keeps me from singing my writer's song loud and flagrantly in the faces of all who come into contact with me.

The fact is, I never thought to pursue my love of writing as a career. I never considered being happy that way, and did not feel that I deserved that kind of happiness. I write that because I, much like many of us, have emotional and psychological blocks on the path towards writing.

SOME OF THOSE blocks come from childhood trauma. As a small child, I was molested by a family member, someone a few years older than me. I am pained and apprehensive writing this, and I still feel guilty implicating someone else, but I think releasing that guilt is important.

What happened to me often feels like this great big weight that has held me down, drowning my intuition, for much of my life. My abuse went on for some time, and I was too afraid to tell anyone. My abuser threatened me that if anyone found out she would blame me, and tell everyone I made her do it. I felt cornered; like I wanted protection and help, but I could not ask for it. I was four, and then five years old. That forced silence is what stuck with me more than anything as I grew up.

I've written many different, private explanations of these events. Explanations for why I am not connected to my whole self. Explanations that are fictional and involve wild animals and the magical surreality of being a person who was sexually molested as a child but is also so many other heroic things that she forgets about it.

Sometimes the event feels like a blackout or a complete dark spot in my memory so that I carry it around but I cannot actually feel it. Its details are hazy, but it's always there, like a secret room in a big house. It has the power to be so many things, but is also one real experience that I often judge "from the outside" as not extreme enough to be the boogeyman that it represents for me on the inside.

Only in my thirties have I come to accept my behavior as a natural reaction to trauma. All of these stories I told myself were for protection. This is a part of what the brain does to protect itself from having to face real fear, harm, and loss of control.

In Johann Hari's book *Lost Connections: Uncovering the Real Causes of Depression — And the Unexpected Solutions*, he talks about feeling responsible, as a child, for abuse. He theorizes that by taking responsibility we take control over events in our lives that we have no control over. His line goes something like, if it is under your control, then it is your fault, and if it is your fault, then you must deserve it. This story, he writes, makes us feel some power. And that is true.

But I also think we tell ourselves a story to plainly make sense of what is happening. Maybe that is for power, but it also happens because our brains construct stories. Rationalizations. Explanations. Myths. We then live by these myths and then either understand or misunderstand the world because of them. That is what we humans do.

AS A STORYTELLER of my own myth, I developed deep guilt, shame, and denial and incorporated that into my sense of self. I stopped listening to my soul. That sacred drum beat I once heard, the one that marked particular steps towards a path as the *right* path, went away. This silence is my theory of why I never followed my writing, or why I never thought to share my words beyond a few friends. I could not hear my intuition.

For a time I thought of my childhood trauma as a "Horcrux" because it cut me off from that part of myself. What if through the energetic impression of trauma (and not the choice to commit an act of violence), we develop accidental, mangled versions of ourselves lying in wait to arise again at some future point? This description helped for a time, as it described dark magic without being too emotionally heavy. I could put it on a shelf and manage it. I could also make it small by picturing it the size of a ring, or a cup.

That is the thing about Horcruxes though. They appear small, and may have started as something of a particular size and shape, but they pick up strength. As a young girl I developed a lot of anxiety. I questioned everything about my interactions with others, and I was very quiet. I was also afraid. I felt so aberrant compared to other people; felt that if people really knew me they would not love me. In this way, my initial trauma consumed shame and was strengthened by it, growing larger towards self-denial and suppression.

THIS SUPPRESSION then expressed itself through all sorts of outlets because what I had really suppressed was my intuition. In this way, the definition for the verb "suppress" as "to put down by authority or force" seems fitting.[1] Additional meanings inform this process, the process of what happens inside a person: "to keep from public knowledge as a: a secret" or "to exclude from consciousness", "to press down", "to restrain from a usual course of action" and "to inhibit the growth or development of."[2] The final entry listed goes beyond skin and bones – "to inhibit the genetic expression of."[3]

A FEW YEARS back I heard a story of rattlesnakes born in the Black Hills of South Dakota with atrophied tail muscles. Now normally, rattlesnakes develop muscles around their rattler as they grow so they can shake it and keep predators away. One scientific theory was that the snakes passed down this genetic defect to avoid predators. By not developing a tail muscle they stayed silent, and also alive. In that same way, people who experience traumatic events at an early age (or at any age), often incorporate denial and suppression into their lifestyles so they can continue on. This can pass down from generation to generation. We let trauma, and the memory of trauma, tell us not to grow. We let it tell us to stay silent, and to survive. I suppressed my intuitive love for writing because it is the loudest thing about me, the thing that makes me feel most like myself, and connects me to the divine.

Without that connection, I grew into an unsure adult. I never felt wholly unconnected from this world but without the acknowledgment and use of creative writing in my life, I was unhappy. In my twenties my unhappiness grew in my new career as a lawyer, in my relationships with other people, and in my body as chronic physical pain. After law school I developed a chronic stress injury in my neck and shoulder that still comes calling on bad days. That injury was another signal, another symptom of something greater, but I couldn't see it. Instead I kept on moving in a direction without hearing my creativity. Without hearing the beat.

HERE AND THERE I heard the faint rhythm, as in a few years later when I took a "community and personal enrichment" creative writing class. Once a week for two months I went to a night class after work where we wrote poems, stories, greeting cards, songs, and anything else not nailed down. No one really read my writing, nor did they particularly care when I read aloud, but the fact that I was generating content felt electric.

I remember an assignment that asked us to explain where we saw our writing in five years and I wrote something about going back to graduate school. My teacher returned the assignment with a note that read, "You don't need more school. You just need to write."

. . .

MONTHS later I was home sick with the flu and I lay on the couch reading *And the Band Played On* by Randy Shilts. I mention this specifically because A) *And the Band Played On* is brilliant and B) it was while reading this that I realized how much I did not like my life.

Randy Shilts was a *San Francisco Chronicle* reporter and tracked years of information into a story that is both medical thriller and human tragedy. Although I can't quite articulate it, *And the Band Played On* helped me take my blinders off. It was a turning point for me, and I could suddenly see my life as not aligning with my desires. I was almost thirty years old and I thought, "My life sucks."

FROM THERE I made an effort to realign over a time period of two years. I did this with yoga and meditation, by connecting with people, spending time in the natural world, reading, and writing. This process was not perfect and is ongoing. At times, it is rocky. I have had bouts of depression and intense anxiety. Throughout it all though, I consult my intuition. I can actually hear my own voice in all of this, and she sings to the beat of a most legitimate drum.

Last year I used this voice to *talk* about writing. I connected with people over it. I went to local writing groups, joined online challenges, and found a group of women to cheerlead with over writing projects. Then this year one of those women asked for stories about why we writers so often feel like we do not deserve to do what we love most.

AT THIS POINT, calling my childhood trauma a Horcrux does not work anymore. Where it once represented a sharp divide or a lost and shattered piece of myself, it is now something that happened when I was a child. So that rather than vanquishing a beast, or being "done" with the terrible thing, I am reabsorbing all of it back into my sense of self. I am metabolizing it, breaking it down, little by little, because I've got other heroic things to do. Like write.

25

THE OUBLIETTE OF OBSIDIAN
ASHLEY EBERST

Maybe you became a mom at the sprightly age of twenty, and while the high school days have long since passed; college has become a dream deferred. However, you continue to read voraciously and still find time to keep a journal on your daily domestic escapades. What better way to retain cherished first moments and memories? What better way to let go of anxieties then to let them bleed out upon the page?

Maybe a decade later you decide now is the time to pursue a bachelors degree. You decide it's time to leave the various healthcare positions you've maintained, and pursue a degree in what you love. You set your sails at full mast because English is something you've always loved, and not to toot your proverbial horn too loud, but you've had a decent knack for it in the past. Maybe it's because when you love to do something you put your whole heart into it. Writing and reading are personal. Your heart and my mind; or my heart and your mind, are engaging in a conversation and relationship, sometimes years and centuries apart. Our symbiotic relationship is a handshake, or perhaps an embrace, and it's incredibly personal. At times it can mold futures and mend heartaches and traumas of the past. It is the language of humanity arcing through time and space.

THROUGH ALL THIS THOUGH, you find that the support for pursuing writing or studying the English major is not always forthcoming. Many times the first inquiry past a pair of plump, prudent lips is: "An English degree? Well what on Earth do you plan on doing with that?" Or perhaps; "Why don't you pursue a degree in the fields of math or science? The STEM pathway is where the future and the money are." This sentiment also holds true in the education of our youth today. A paradigm shift from the humanities and the arts whose benefits were once praised among the intellectuals and the philosophers has come into fruition.

Through all this, why write? Why suffer the criticism, the self-loathing, and the rejections? There may be no money, no chance of being published, and there will always be derision from one corner or another. Why?

Write because to not write is to let the words written on your soul sink into an oubliette of obsidian. Write because there are always words that need to be written, now more than ever. Write because even if there is no money in it, the act and the product are still profitable. Write because it provides clarity for a conglomeration of thoughts and emotions that might otherwise not ever rise to the surface. Write because even if no one else reads it, there is still profound meaning in it.

NEVER STOP WRITING. To stop writing is to isolate the

threads in the web of humanity. To stop writing is akin to locking up the emotions and thoughts that need to be realized. To stop writing is to lose a part of oneself. To stop writing is to silence a part of the soul.

Write the words that are etched on your heart and soul, so that they can take shape and imprint on another. Words and books can be balms for the soul. Being a part of the writing process connects you on a divine level with the beginnings of humanity and expression.

Letter by letter, word by word, sentence by sentence, these stories bind us together and as we internalize them provide us with structure. Think of all the stories that have made a difference. What we need now more than ever is a *difference*. We need caring. We need balms for the heart and soul. Don't let the lights go out, and the words and stories fall into the oubliette of obsidian.

26

THE ROAD ACTUALLY TAKEN

GABRIELA PEREIRA

Last summer, I took an arts and literature pilgrimage to the Berkshires where I visited the homes of creative heroes like Edith Wharton, Herman Melville, Norman Rockwell, and Robert Frost. As I wandered through their studios and homes, I wondered: "Did these people choose their path, or was it chosen for them?"

In their own way, each of these artists and authors tackle this very same issue in their work. Edith Wharton's short story *Roman Holiday*, for example, asks whether a person's destiny is shaped by her circumstances or through the choices that she makes. Melville's *Moby Dick* is all about the lengths people are willing to go to when chasing a "great white whale" in their own lives, no matter how dangerous—or deadly—it may be.

NORMAN ROCKWELL'S WORK, on the other hand, might come across as nostalgic slices of Americana on the surface, but when you look at his career as a whole, you see a very different story. He makes deliberate artistic choices to depict individuals in less than glamorous circumstances and tackle hot-button issues like integration and war. His pseudo self-portrait "Blank Canvas" (October 8, 1938) and the later "Triple Self-Portrait" (February 13, 1960), which is a visual echo of the former, are pictures of an artist grappling with his responsibility to portray the world as he truly sees it.

AND THEN, of course, we have Robert Frost, author of one of the most misunderstood poems of all time. I remember reading "The Road Not Taken" in high school and feeling as though the poet had opened a window into my very soul. I memorized that poem, murmured it under my breath when the mean girls at school said nasty things to me. Whenever something in my life did not go my way, I would cling to those last two lines like a talisman:

I took the road less traveled by,
And that has made all the difference.

At the time I interpreted the poem the way the way movies like *Dead Poets Society* made us believe it was intended. Forge your own path! Find your own destiny! As long as you're true to yourself, greatness will come.

But what no one ever tells you is that greatness often has a cost.

IN MY EARLY teens I discovered I had superpowers. I'm not talking about comic book powers like the ability to fly or turn invisible. No, my superpowers were a bit more mundane, but in many ways no less dangerous and terrifying. I discovered that I could go days—even weeks—with barely more than an hour or two of sleep each night, and I didn't feel tired.

I'd wake up at two or three o'clock in the morning, like an alarm had gone off in my head, and since I shared a room with my younger sister and lying awake in the dark is *boring*, I realized early on that I'd need to find a productive way to use that time. I'd tiptoe to the kitchen, the only room in our Manhattan apartment where turning on the lights wouldn't wake everybody in my family, and I'd work. I finished homework assignments months ahead of time. I read dozens of books. I kept a journal filled with terrible, self-indulgent poetry. I drew cartoons.

THIS ROUTINE STARTED as a way to stave off boredom but I quickly discovered that it was also necessary for my own survival. Almost as quickly as those superpowers emerged, they disappeared again. It was like I had been hit by a dose of my own personal kryptonite, only it wouldn't just take away that go-go-go frenetic energy, it would also sap me of my very will to live. At this moment, there was nothing else to do but huddle down into this secret cave inside my soul. I didn't work. I didn't talk. I didn't even think.

Then, BING! My superpowers would turn back on and I'd be running a mile a minute again. I realized that if I wanted to counteract those kryptonite moments, I'd have to hustle as hard as I could while my superpowers worked. Eventually, I found a rhythm, if you could call it that; most days it felt like I was dancing to music that couldn't decide if it was a polka or samba. I'd work hard for days, weeks, even months, only to brace myself for the crash lurking just over the crest of the hill. Once that crash happened—and it always did—I knew I only had one job: survive until my powers came back.

THINGS GOT a lot easier in college. Campus life was surprisingly compatible with my erratic, up-and-down existence. It's easy to mask a mental illness when you have no serious responsibilities or pesky parents asking questions. By the time I graduated, I had perfected "playing sane" to an art form. I got so good at it that even when I sought help from all eight campus shrinks—hoping against hope that one of them might be able to figure out what was wrong with me—not a single one of them could. According to them, I was perfectly normal.

Except, "normal" people don't end up in the psychiatric ward.

From then on, I led a double life. Every morning I donned my mask and became the mild-mannered, put-together version of myself that everyone expected to see. Most of the time I lived up to that persona, but the few times that the mask came down, the reality people saw was powerful, ferocious, and terrifying. Most of the time, though, I was able to keep "the beast" under wraps.

GRADUATION WAS when the trouble started. The "real world" isn't nearly as forgiving of mental illness as college or graduate school can be. I discovered that bosses don't like it when you disappear for days or weeks at a time, even if it's because you're in the emergency room. Plus, the minute you tell someone you went to the hospital, they're going to ask you why. With all the stigma surrounding mental illness, you can bet I wasn't opening that door, at least not at that time in my life. I kept my mouth shut and for all my boss or coworkers knew, every time I disappeared I just was taking personal days to go shopping.

During this period, my psychiatrist and I tested every possible medication for bipolar disorder. (You're welcome, pharmaceutical industry.) This process of trial-and-error lasted two and a half years. I remember trying one drug that was great at first, until I lost the ability form coherent speech. Given that my job at the time involved talking (as most jobs do) we promptly eliminated this option. Then there was this new miracle pill with no known side-effects, except for this rare but lethal rash affecting only .01% of the population. Guess who was that special snowflake.

Eventually we landed on a solution that kept me sane, allowed me to be functional, and didn't kill me with the side effects. The only downside was that it dulled my reflexes, making it no longer safe for me to drive a car. For a girl living in Manhattan, not driving was no big deal. But my job at the time was in New Jersey, and the only public transportation took three hours. Each way.

THE WEEK I quit that job is still a blur. I remember acing my annual review. I remember my boss promoting me. I remember being selected to accompany a few key team members to visit our manufacturers in China. And then I remember being in the emergency room, about to die. The day I returned from the hospital, I gave my two-weeks notice. It wasn't easy choosing my medication over my job, but survival is a strong instinct.

FOR YEARS I resented my mental illness. I hated that I had to give up a career that I not only loved, but that I excelled at. For years I refused to update my LinkedIn profile (or even log in) because it brought up so much shame. I kept asking myself why having a job—heck, staying alive—had to be so freaking hard when everyone else made it look so effortless. Then I realized all this sturm und drang wasn't doing me any good. It was time for me to stop whining and start building something else. That's when writing came into my life.

MANY PEOPLE SEE what I've created through my writing and DIY MFA as though it's something impressive. Don't get me wrong; I love my work, I love writing, and I love the company I've built. I'm glad things turned out the way they did. But this wasn't my first choice. It was the runner-up option.

People have this misguided notion that writing is a somehow voluntary. I'm sure there are some people who proactively choose to be writers, but for others writing chooses *them*, like the career equivalent of a sorting hat ceremony. And then there are people like me, who don't have the luxury of any choice. We end up as writers because our personal demons will not allow us to hold down any other type of job. We have to play the cards we are dealt.

I FINALLY CAME to terms with all of this when I watched a Disney princess movie and saw my life—my very *self*—reflected on the screen. This realization was especially odd because I was never into the princess thing as a child. If you asked four-year-old me what I thought of princess movies, I'd have told you that randomly breaking into song and talking to woodland animals was pretty weird. Plus, I didn't want to sit around waiting for a "prince" to swoop in and rescue me. *I* wanted to slay dragons and conquer lands far and wide. And when the battles were over, I would run my mighty empire like a well-oiled machine.

This is why, when I saw the movie *Frozen* I wasn't just alarmed at how deeply I empathized with the story, but also at how I could see my life encapsulated by a princess with crazy ice powers. Just as Elsa's ice magic was both beautiful and dangerous, so too was my own brand of superpower.

Elsa spends her childhood learning to "conceal, don't feel" and I spent most of my young adulthood training myself to "play normal," the way you might train a dog to roll over and play dead. Like Elsa, isolation was my ally. For a long time it was the only way to keep the people close to me safe from a demon I couldn't control.

Yet, as I watched the movie I realized something: Fearing the beast and shutting it away is not how you control it. The more Elsa tries to clamp down her powers, the stronger and more violent they become. It was only when she channeled her powers through love that she was able to regain control.

Love.

Love is hard. Like last week, when a guy cut in front of me while getting on the Q train and grabbed the last empty seat (even though I had a three-year-old in tow), it was hard to extend compassion and not secretly curse that jerk under my breath.

Speaking of children, there are certainly times when it's very difficult for me to love my own two munchkins, especially when it's four hours past their bedtime, and they ask for a glass of water… for the seventeenth time. Sometimes it's even hard to love my job, because even the best job in the world can drive you crazy once in a while.

But the hardest thing to love is mental illness. Let's face it, there's not much that's lovable about my bipolar disorder. It has caused me to burn bridges and ruin relationships, despite my best attempts at the contrary. It has almost killed me on at least four different occasions and I live with the constant fear that in the end I won't kick the bucket of natural causes, but because this illness will get me first. Bipolar also forced me to give up a job I loved and abandon a career I had worked for during most of my young adult life. And yet, if it weren't for this illness, I would never have left my job in the toy industry to become a writer, and I would never have founded DIY MFA.

This path is certainly not the one I intended. My childhood dream was to be a toy designer, not the founder of an education company, and yet the two things are not too far apart. In fact, as I reflect on everything I learned and all the skills I developed as I worked toward my "dream job," this is the same knowledge base and skillset I draw from every day for my current work.

There's this romantic notion that writers have always been writers "for as long as they can remember," and while I can certainly look back on my childhood and teenage years and identify the early seeds of my current career, the truth is that it doesn't really matter whether this path was the one I intended or not. This is the road I am on now, which brings me back to our literary friends: Wharton, Melville, Rockwell, and Frost.

As writers and artists we often romanticize the road not taken, regretting the opportunities missed or agonizing over those times when we took a path that led us away from our goal.

Destiny is like a heavy fog. It may seem real, even to the point where it can distort how we see the path that lies ahead of us, but it has no real substance. I think too many writers spend their time worrying about the past or wondering about the future.

Yet the only moment that is truly *real* is the one we're in right now. Instead of desperately trying to hold onto something that has no substance, we must do what Elsa does in *Frozen*. The only way to reach our so-called destiny is to "let it go" and fully embrace the path that we're on and the moment we're in right now.

27

MY ALMOST SECRET WRITING LIFE
TAMMY L. BREITWEISER

Everyone enjoys the feeling of belonging, especially to an exclusive club. The privilege that comes with being part of an inner circle feeds the ego and self image. It is similar to being part of the wedding party or the 1% of people who run a marathon. Not everyone can do it, but when you do you have insider information and importance on your side.

I have been part of a secret society of one for most of my life. I am a writer.

THIS LABEL of writer has not adhered to me easily. It is like a sticker that has been pulled off too many times in a panic and loses its integrity. The last couple of months has marked a period of transition dealing with my personal title. The imposter syndrome and the inner critics have been muffled and I have started to utter and refer to myself as a genuine writer. Proclaiming the label writer on my social media platforms has made it a public step. I have many personal obstacles to believing the statement, *I am a writer,* even though I continually get words on the page, digital and analog.

THE COMPULSION TO write began when I was 8 or 9 years old . Writing has always been a constant. At times of transition such as marriage, divorce, remarriage and graduations the words have roused me from sleep and demanded to be recorded. Many pages have been written in a half-awake trance early in the morning.

Throughout school, my favorite assignments were essays. In third grade, I was chosen for a creative writing group that unfortunately only met a few times. I remember the yellow folders and the special feeling, but it didn't last. I always worried that I had done something wrong, or didn't write well enough which caused the cessation. A respected teacher praised my description in a fifth grade essay, but the act of writing was always just a hobby even though I spent a lot of time doing it. If I wasn't reading, I was writing. It was just something I did.

In high school, I was forced to do an outline for a response to Macbeth. I was praised for the organization of this essay. The little feedback I received was not enough to make me a better writer. I read voraciously but never had anyone really make the connection that I could learn to be a better writer from reading. I didn't know how to take what I knew about reading a good story and make actionable steps to transfer to the written word.

I desperately wanted feedback and to be a better writer but wasn't able to find much help. Every time it seemed I would get some feedback the opportunity would fizzle out. Looking back now, I wonder if I sabotaged some of these experiences because I was afraid.

. . .

My parents discouraged writing as a career. The memory is hazy about exactly how, as memories often play out. "That really isn't a real job" were words that were uttered.

My best friend in college was a creative writing major. Her thesis was a chapbook of poetry. I lived through her wishing that I had had the courage to take creative writing classes. I considered it a hobby and I shared very little writing with anyone. I wrote a few essays for scholarships but my voice was not in them. At the time I didn't know that was what was wrong.

I read *Wild Mind* by Natalie Goldberg and did the writing exercises. When I was reading it waiting for a linguistics class to begin, a classmate came up to me and asked what class I was reading the book for. I told her it wasn't for a class, I was just reading it. She walked away asking "Why?!" In her mind, it was incredulous to read a writing book for fun .

For undergraduate work, I pursued a degree in elementary education with a reading concentration. I dreamed of becoming the reading and writing teacher I longed to have when I was a child. In my own classrooms, I facilitated daily writing opportunities. I wrote with my students and fostered a love of reading and writing.

There are past students I have conversed with that still have the little books they wrote as authors in my classroom. The writing projects that were so important to them in first grade are still important to them as adults. Studying the process of writing for teaching was my excuse and drive. I did not feel justified in studying it for a personal or professional pursuit at that time in my life.

I was always reading a writing book, which aided me to learn more to help my students.

I HAVE COLLECTED novel false starts like dust bunnies under my bed. Several years ago, I wrote the beginning to a third novel and had the nerve to share it with one high school English teacher I knew. He gave me some constructive feedback but it was discouraging. The story wasn't working and I knew it, but I didn't know how to fix it and neither did he.

Last fall, I dedicated time to writing in my daily schedule. I wrote one short per day. My self-imposed rules were simple: I needed to write a story with a beginning, middle, and end. The rule was to complete the story. After about 5 days the stories started to improve.

I read more short stories and used mentor texts. I researched university writing courses and downloaded the syllabi and ordered the books recommended for study.

The next step became participating in National Novel Writing Month (affectionately called NANOWRIMO) and over the course of November, 50,000 words of short stories appeared in my Google drive. Revision is a process, and I am still creating as I am inspired.

NO REAL-LIFE WRITERS are within my circle of concern. I have a beta reader that is a voracious reader and knows good story, which is valuable. An online writing and critique group in Scribophile allows me the feedback to improve my craft. Serious writers critique work for points. The accumulated points allow your own work to be critiqued. The comments are helpful and encouraging and push my thinking.

To be published I have to send writing out. I set goals for submissions monthly. I strive to accumulate a wall of rejections...and acceptances. I have a few acceptances in my portfolio. The hurtle is the mindset that my writing is only for me. Using that excuse is a crutch to avoid the pain of rejection. Without rejection, I cannot accept the joy of acceptance. I must be vulnerable.

IF I COULD GO BACK in time I wish that I would have taken more creative writing classes in college. If I win the lottery I will go back and get my MFA. Often I feel I do not deserve the label of writer without this degree. The debate is ongoing of the benefits but I feel an MFA from Iowa would be an accomplishment. For now, I develop and deploy my independent study. The community was the largest obstacle for the longest time. My skill has increased so I mostly feel my work is worthy of reading

Although it was secret to everyone but me, I wrote all the time, all these years. I would say it was just for me. I would say it was to know what I am thinking. I would say I would write to vent and to make decisions.

In these moments, there were amazing phrases I was happy I wrote even though I was not expecting it. The form was usually an essay, journal entry or poem.

My writer's notebook is with me at all times. The scribbles and notes are collections of ideas, snippets of language and story which are fuel for the more public writer I am now.

Despite all the obstacles, either external or self-imposed, the writing wins. Writing is my constant, forever.

28

EMOTIONAL CONSTIPATION
J. DAVID

The time was ripe.

I'd been following the #metoo stories of women who'd courageously spoken up about the violation of their bodies. As one woman after another came forward in the news, I couldn't help but remember my own experience with sexual assault.

For years I felt ashamed and tried to forget what happened. But listening to other women's stories brought memories back up to the surface. It was deeply unsettling. Yet hearing them made me feel less alone.

In some way, their stories healed me.

I felt inspired to tell my own story. Perhaps sharing it would help someone else.

But since it happened so long ago, I had to conjure up details and memories. I skimmed through my old diaries. I rummaged through boxes searching for pictures of myself as a shy schoolgirl. I even listened to old songs from that time – the ones that made me want to sing along when they played on the radio:

Hey Mickey you're so fine, you're so fine you blow my mind, hey Mickey, hey Mickey!

Whenever I found evidence - a school photo or a few faded sentences in a diary- I felt a little pang of excitement, followed by a thud in the pit of my stomach.

Grief and anger welled up with each memory, but I pushed them away with my mind.

"Get it together - you can do this," I assured myself. After all, it happened so long ago. And time heals all wounds - doesn't it?

After a few days of 'research', I was finally ready to face the blank page.

But the day I'd planned to start, I suddenly became ill. Instead of writing at my desk, I was hunched over the toilet, violently puking.

It didn't stop.

For the next 48 hours I crawled between my bed and the bathroom, stomach twisted up in knots.

MY WISE FRIEND Janice called to check on me.

"So, what brought on this stomach flu?" she asked. "I mean, besides the food you ate - what's upsetting you?"

I told her about my writing project. Perhaps facing my past filled me with more dread than I dared to admit.

"Maybe it's not a good time to do this. If I were you, I'd wait until you're feeling better," she said.

She had a point.

. . .

But on the other hand, I wondered – is there *ever* a good time to write a painful story?

The thing is, when it's time for stories to be told, they push up against your insides until you're so uncomfortable they simply *must* come out.

And although part of me wanted to do it, the other half of me resisted:

"You need to tell this story."

"But I don't want to talk about it – what will people think if they find out?"

"You might help someone else if you share it."

"Who cares what happened to me? Everybody has a #metoo story these days."

"But YOUR experience matters, too."

"Can't I just leave this in the past where it belongs?"

Maybe the stomach flu was my body's way of processing all those conflicted thoughts and painful emotions.

Still, the story didn't care. It wanted to be told.

And I had nothing else to do while I recovered in bed.

I already felt miserable, so why not write it anyway?

I soldiered on and picked up my pen.

I'd barely written three sentences before wanting to run away. I dragged myself out of bed to look out the window, wishing I could go outside and let the cold winter wind blow my anxiety away. But I couldn't leave the house – I was still too sick.

I managed to write a few more words before the lump in my throat threatened to rise up and explode into tears. I quickly nipped it in the bud with a sudden urge to shop for new shoes online.

. . .

Two hours later, the page was still there, waiting patiently for me.

I couldn't even reach for food, my usual buffer for dealing with stress. I'd just throw it back up. \

It was clear that no matter how many times I distracted myself, the page wasn't going anywhere.

And neither was I.

The only way out of this was *through* it – I had to finish what I'd started.

"Breathe," I said to myself. *"Pretend you're writing about someone else. Think about how much better you'll feel once it's done."*

After a day and a half, I finally finished the first draft of my story.

Deep sigh of relief. The hardest part was over.

Editing would be another hurdle, but at least the story was on the page.

Strangely, when I woke up the next morning, I felt lighter – as though a burden was lifted off my shoulders.

And I could eat again! Plain rice never tasted so delicious.

In three days, I'd purged so much more than toxins from my system.

I released the emotional constipation that my body had, for so long, carried in shame.

And finally, I felt free to move on.

29

A LINED ESCAPE

TARA CALIHMAN

It had been ages since a stranger hit on me. Of course, it was at a bar when I was keeping to myself, attempting to write amid the noise and distraction of an Irish funeral. He was extremely drunk and wouldn't be swayed from his objective. I gave many indications of not wanting to talk, of being busy, otherwise engaged.

But he was persistent, spewing stories and asking questions. Every time he ordered another pint, I put my head down, scribbling a few sentences where I could. I finished an entire paragraph while he was out smoking a cigarette. He wanted to know about my writing, his ex-wife was a writer, I shook my head and wrote it anyway.

HE DIDN'T like it when I wrote in the notebook. It was my refuge, my safe space. I didn't have any friends, so the notebook became the place where I could express my doubts about the marriage, my confusion about what was happening and my fear about the future. The notebook came with me everywhere.

When we would get in a fight, he would use the notebook against me. Telling me that I would never be a writer, that I would never have the strength to leave him, that I was crazy for having dreams. It took many years and a series of notebooks to work up the courage to change my story. I look at those scribblings now as a reflection of my 20s...hurried, messy, and trying to figure it out as I go along. It's hard to read but I'm so happy that I wrote it anyway.

Is that supposed to be a joke? Are you trying to be funny? Have you been to grad school? Do you know anyone in L.A.? What do you know about writing screenplays? Are you getting paid yet? What are you writing? Who do you think you are? Are you still writing those things? How many rejections are you up to now? Are you invested in this company? Is this just a day job? How many competitions are you going to enter? Have you taken any classes?

IF IT'S NOT a drunk man, then it's a disapproving parent, a doubtful colleague or a skeptical stranger. I don't need to worry about the voice in my head. There are enough people questioning what I do, asking about the plan, wondering when I'll give up.

But I keep writing. For my sanity. For my son. For my future and for my past.

I wrote it when I didn't think I could. I wrote it when I couldn't say it out loud. I wrote it because I didn't know what else to do. I wrote it because I had no other choice.

CONTRIBUTORS

Michelle Ainslie

Michelle Ainslie is currently completing an MA in Creative Writing and her first collection of poetry was published in January 2018. She has chosen to swim upstream and build her life around words. At the moment this translates into being a freelance editor, writing coach and author. She lives in Cape Town with her two cats. www.micha.co.za

Jazmine Aluma

Jazmine Aluma writes in response to fear, and as a way to figure out the how to move forward. During the day she is a ghostwriter, editor, and copywriter. At night she is a blogger and memoirist. Her writing has been seen in The Huffington Post, Bust.com, LA Weekly and LA Yoga magazine, among others. She is currently writing a memoir in between night feedings, shuffling her preschooler around town, and working full time. She lives and plays in Chicago with her two cats, two kids, and husband. writinginbold.com

Claire Basarich

Claire Basarich is a writer, translator, editor/proofreader, and language teacher. A French-American dual national, she was born and raised in Atlanta, Georgia and has been living in England for 7 years. Her work has been published in *Barcelona Ink*, *El Libro Rojo*, *5 by Five Writers*, and *Now Then Magazine*, among others. Her poetry has been longlisted for the Rialto Nature & Place Prize 2017 and the Live Canon 2018 International Poetry Competition, and her short story "Underground" was awarded 2nd place in the Splintered Lip Story Competition, shortlisted for the Eyelands 8th International Short Story Competition 2018, and performed on Radio Sheffield (2017). Claire has read at events including the Barcelona Poetry Brothel, Sheffield WordLife, Sheffield Poem-a-thon for asylum seekers, the Off the Shelf Literary Festival, and the Bowery Poetry Club in NYC. You can contact Claire for language-related projects
here: http://clairebasarich.wix.com/clairebasarich

Tammy Breitweiser

Tammy L. Breitweiser is a writer living in the Midwest and working on her first collection of short stories. Her poetry has been published in The Storyteller Magazine and her flash fiction in The Ninja Writers Monthly. You can connect with Tammy through her blog https://tammysreadinglife.wordpress.com/

Tara Calihman

Tara Calihman is a expat writer and comedian, living in Ireland and desperately seeking good Mexican food in Dublin. She can most often be found on her bike, on the trail or in a book. Her work has been published on The Cooper Review, Blunt Moms and neutrons/protons. https://www.taracalihman.com/

Terri Connellan

Terri Connellan lives in Sydney, Australia and is a writer and life coach at Quiet Writing, specialising in creativity and self-leadership. Certified in personality type assessment based on Jung/Myers-Briggs theory, Terri celebrates and explores personal narratives for creative living. As a life coach, she guides women through deeper self-understanding of their body of work, personality strengths and unique passions to shape a more wholehearted story, especially in times of transition.

With a background in adult literacy teaching and qualifications to Masters' level in Language and Literacy, Terri is a published poet and author of '36 Books that Shaped my Story: Reading as Creative Influence'. An avid blogger, guest-blogger and feature writer, including for inspired COACH Magazine, she writes on topics as diverse as personality type, introversion, neuroscience, leadership, self-leadership, creativity, writing, productivity, tarot and books for emerging coaches. http://www.quietwriting.com/

J. David

J. David is a holistic wellness practitioner and artist. For as long as she can remember, she has always turned to writing as a way to make sense of the world, heal emotional wounds and access her inner guidance. She aspires to help others do the same through her healing practice.

J. lives in New York with her partner, feline boss and a vast collection of tarot cards.

Kalyani Deshpande

Kalyani Deshpande writes thought-provoking, cross-cultural stories that uplift and inspire. Her work is shaped by her experiences of living in Africa, India and now, the United States. Kalyani has completed one novel, *The Year of Yes* and is currently working on a collection of magical realism short stories. She has been a finalist in North Carolina State University's Short Story Contest.

Kalyani lives in the San Francisco Bay Area with her husband and two sons and works as a UX Designer. Learn more about her here: kalyanideshpande.com

Caroline Donahue

Caroline Donahue is a writer, writing coach, and podcast host living in Berlin. She is the Co-Creator of the anthology, I Wrote it Anyway and the creator and host of The Secret Library Podcast. She is currently at work on her first novel. She can be found online at carolinedonahue.com.

Ashley Eberst

Ashley dwells in the rather ordinary but lovely Midwest with her amazing husband, kids, and two grouchy cats. She has spent over a decade working in healthcare; including but not limited to the fields of hospice, otolaryngology, pediatric and emergency medicine. While she has enjoyed these rewarding endeavors, she wants to try her hand (literally) at what she really loves, which is writing. Currently she tutors college students in writing; helping them to find their respective voices and hone their craft. When she isn't reading or writing she can be found traveling, engaging in culinary adventures, and spending copious amounts of time with her children while they are still in their youth. She can be found online at twitter.com/a_eberst.

Clementine Ewokolo-Burnley

Clementine Ewokolo-Burnley is a writer, mother and community worker. Her poems and short fiction have appeared in the Bristol Short Story Prize Anthology 2017, LossLit Magazine, die Neue Rundschau, the Emma Press Poems about Britain, and elsewhere. She makes jam and isn't the most fun person at dinner parties, especially when she talks about how power dynamics influence social change strategies. You can find her online at clementineeburnley.com

Frodot

When asked what I do, my usual answer ... a system engineer since most work is technical. But other roles included marketing, advertising, and management. I call myself a writer not because I got paid for it sometimes but rather because I love to arrange words into ideas.

Our family moved a lot when I grew up 'here and there'; so it was a natural path in later life. Lived in a couple of countries and several states in the USA. Worked and visited more but have not seen enough. Family remains a central part of who I am. Family like the systems created are scattered around the world. I can be found @todorf on Instagram.

Melissa Fu

Melissa Fu grew up in Northern New Mexico and moved to Cambridge, UK in 2006. She earned a BA in Physics and English at Rice University, followed by an MS in Physics from the University of Colorado and an MA in English Education at Teachers College, Columbia University. Prior to focusing on writing, she worked as an outreach coordinator, classroom teacher, and independent consultant. In 2014, she combined her loves of teaching and writing to start Spilling the Ink, a small business offering creative writing courses and coaching.

Melissa was the regional winner of the Words and Women 2016 Prose Competition and was a 2017 Apprentice with the London-based Word Factory. She has been awarded the 2019/2019 David T.K. Wong Creative Writing Fellowship at the University of East Anglia. Melissa's writing appears in several publications including *The Lonely Crowd, International Literature Showcase, Bare Fiction, Wasafiri Online,* and *Words and Women.* spillingtheink.com

Valerie Griffin

Valerie lives by the sea in Dorset. She belongs to two writing groups and likes to attend writing festivals and retreats to hone her writing skills and meet other writers. She has won a couple of short story competitions, been runner up and has had short stories and flash fictions published online and in print anthologies. Valerie is also an avid letter writer with plenty to say. Hobbies include reading for at least an hour every day (various genres as long as it's readable), gardening and inadvertently growing weird shaped vegetables and people watching on the seafront. She is currently researching and working on her first novel. You can find Valerie on Twitter @griffin399.

Claire Harnett Mann

Claire Harnett-Mann teaches English and literacy to refugee and migrant communities in Birmingham, UK. She has a BA in English Language and Literature, has studied both Gender and Education at postgraduate level, and is now undertaking an MA in Creative Writing at the Open University. Her poetry has been published in The Rialto and Magma magazines, and she is at present writing a novel about a survivor of psychological abuse who uses creative writing as a pathway to healing and self-realisation.

Alongside her writing, Claire's biggest passions are tarot, intersectional feminism and kitchen witchery. She changes the colour of her nail varnish with every new moon cycle and is currently engaged in regular shadow work with a local canal side heron. Come say hello at https://claireharnettmann.com

Hannah Howard

Hannah Howard is a writer and food expert who spent her formative years eating, drinking, serving, bartending, cooking on a hot line, flipping giant wheels of cheese, and managing restaurants. She is the author of the memoir Feast: True Love in and Out of the Kitchen. Hannah is a graduate of Columbia University and the Bennington Writing Seminars. She writes for SELF, New York Magazine, and Salon.com, and lives in New York City. hannahhoward.nyc

Erin Jourdan

Erin Jourdan, MFA Creative Writing, is a Los Angeles based writer and teacher. She is the founder of MemoirClass.com LLC, the premier educational source for writing from personal experience on the web. She is the recipient of a 2007 Djerassi Resident Artist Fellowship and a 2009 Jentel Foundation Artist Residency. She teaches memoir/writing from personal experience classes to private clients, workshop groups, MOOCs and through her website www.memoirclass.com.

Rose Ketring

Rose Ketring is a writer, acrylic and collage creator, as well as a mental health advocate. My subject matter is about the power to create new meaning from simple materials. Each collage and painting contains my thoughts, poetry and emotions that whisper prayers. A candle is lit as my hands dip into color and spread across the page in meditation. Shapes gather and move as if they were dancing. Some seem to spring fully formed from my hands in shining Beauty. Others, like puzzle pieces that have been half digested, call forth Resistance.

My written words inform my creative process, drawing inspiration from experiences with depression and anxiety. Connection and self love are very important and life is never taken for granted. Spirituality has been a difficult and wondrous journey leading me through where I am today. I am inspired by my grandma who left this world over ten years ago, Frida Kahlo who refused to be defined through her injuries or her subject matter, and the poet Mary Oliver whose words continue to fill me with beauty and awe. https://www.instagram.com/blurosemd/

Tanya Levy

Tanya Levy, aka heartlady, is a Counsellor, Educator, Writer, Healer, and Digital Artist living in Cape Breton, Nova Scotia. She is a contributor to all the books in the 365 Series created by Jodi Chapman and Dan Tech. These books include: 365 Ways to Connect With Your Soul, 365 Moments of Grace, 365 Life Shifts and Goodness Abounds. Her art is featured in the Oracle Card Deck, Priestesses of the New Earth. She is known for her optimism, intuitions, wisdom and sense of humour. She has worked in the social work field for thirty years. Her hobbies include: writing, Tai Chi, gardening, spending time in nature and taking photos of hearts. You can view her inspirational photography, poetry and writing at https://www.facebook.com/heartladyinspiration.

Kim Manginelli

Kim Manganelli is an associate professor of nineteenth-century British and American literature at Clemson

University and a novelist in progress. She is a Certified Leader of the Amherst Writers and Artists method whose Wisteria Writing Workshops give writers of all levels of education and experience a safe and playful space to get their words out of their heads and onto the page. She currently lives in Greenville, SC but is always dreaming of Paris. Visit her online at wisteriawriters.com.

Gabriela Pereira

Gabriela Pereira is an author, TEDx speaker, and entrepreneur who wants to challenge the status quo of higher education. As the founder and instigator of DIY MFA, her mission is to empower writers, artists and other creatives to take an entrepreneurial approach to their education and professional growth.

Gabriela earned her MFA in writing from The New School and speaks at college campuses and national conferences. She is also the host of DIY MFA Radio, a popular podcast where she interviews bestselling authors and book industry professionals. Gabriela is the author of the book *DIY MFA: Write with Focus, Read with Purpose, Build Your Community* (Writer's Digest Books, 2016), a comprehensive guide to help writers get the MFA experience without going to school. To join the DIY MFA community and get a free Starter Kit, go to DIYMFA.com/join.

Paula Priamos

Paula Priamos is the author of *The Shyster's Daughter: A Memoir* (Etruscan Books) as well as *Inside V* (Rare Bird Books). Her essays and short stories have appeared in *The New York Times Magazine, The Washington Post Magazine, The*

Los Angeles Times Magazine, Crimewave Magazine and *ZYZZY-VA,* among other publications.

Her most recent novel *Inside V* is the Gold Award Winner for a Foreword INDIE Best Book Award for Thriller & Suspense. She teaches English and Creative Writing at California State University, San Bernardino.

David Rocklin

David Rocklin is the author of *The Luminist* and the award-winning The Night Language. He is also the founder/curator of Roar Shack, a monthly reading series in Los Angeles. He was born and raised in Chicago and now lives in LA with his wife, daughters and a 150 lb Great Dane who seriously needs to stay on his own bed. He's currently at work on his next novel, *The Electric Love Song of Fleischl Berger.* Find me on Facebook

Sarah Skovold

Sarah believes creating a life you love is an art form that must be practiced daily. She loves her family, travel, adventure, a variety of artistic endeavors and has a passion for health, physical and mental healing practices to help inspire others to create their best life. Her work involves sharing insights, tools and her personal joys and struggles to help individuals on their personal journey to create a life they love! CreateLoveLive.com

Kate Swindlehurst

Kate Swindlehurst, MA, lives and works in Cambridge, England, where she writes full-time (when she isn't dancing). Diagnosed with Parkinson's in 2004, she is a firm believer in the therapeutic power of Argentine tango and her memoir *Parkinson's & the Tango Effect: my Year on the Dance Floor* is currently funding with award-winning publisher Unbound. Kate's interests include health and well-being generally, both for the individual and as a society, and our relationship with the natural world. A regular blogger, Kate has also completed a novel and two short story collections and has had short stories & non-fiction published in print and online. She is currently working on a novel exploring our attitudes to migration. Read more on her website www.kateswindlehurst.com

Prerna Uppal

Prerna is a former journalist whose work has appeared in leading Indian newspapers, news and feature magazines, as well as on a leading national news network. Her creative non-fiction work as appeared in Nine Lives: a Life in 10 minutes anthology, The Health Collective and the Chicken Soup for the Indian Soul series. Based in London for the last 9 years, she currently works for a disability charity. A cooking enthusiast, you can follow Prerna's kitchen chronicals on www.foodoodle.wordpress.com, and/or if blackout poetry is more your style, you can find her work at @inkpen81

Teri Vela

Teri Vela lives in Las Vegas, Nevada, with her partner Sean. Her poem *Heads or Tails* was published in *Clark: Poetry from Clark County, Nevada* (Zeitgeist Press, 2017). *Rattler* is her first published essay. She is a member of the *She Howls Women's Writing Circle*, led by Dal Kular. She is currently working on anything written, anything read.

Sarah Miller Walters

Sarah Miller Walters has been writing and self-publishing novellas and short story collections since 2012. Her main interest is 20th century social history and much of her work reflects this, focussing on cinema and other past-times. Some might say that her themes are nostalgic, but she likes to challenge the view that the past was a better place to live - particularly if you were a woman.

Her day job involves writing grant applications for local charities in north Derbyshire. She has also been able to begin developing her interest in writing for wellbeing by delivering writing workshops for those accessing the services that she helps to run. These include sessions on journalling and poetry writing for those with chronic and terminal health conditions.

Sarah is currently obsessed with 1950s problem pages in women's magazines and is experimenting with a poetry collection inspired by these. Unfortunately, she can sometimes relate to the problems expressed by these repressed housewives. She can be found on instagram at @adventureswithword

Grace Ward

Grace Ward is a writer living in the UK.

ACKNOWLEDGMENTS

There are so many people to thank who were part of the creation of this book.

First, of course, the contributors. Thank you for sharing your stories. Thank you for being brave and writing anyway.

Thank you to Claire Basarich for editing and proofreading support. You stepped in at a crucial moment and this book would not have been finished without you.

Thank you to Barry McWilliams for being our design hero and creating a cover that we are all so proud of.

Thank you to everyone who has purchased this book and is therefore supporting both Arts Emergency and 826 LA. You are the best.

Copyright © 2018 Caroline Donahue and Dal Kular
All rights reserved.
ISBN:
ISBN-13:

NOTES

24. Rattler

1. 1 *Merriam-Webster's Collegiate Dictionary*, 11th ed., 2011.
2. 2 *Id*
3. 3 Def. 6. *Id.*

www.ingramcontent.com/pod-product-compliance
Lightning Source LLC
Chambersburg PA
CBHW050302010526
44108CB00040B/2065